I0128530

TILMAN RESCH

1st edition

January 2025

SUCCESS FUNDAMENTALS

The 5-Phase System for Ultimate Achievement:
Master Your Mindset, Time, and Results

Your Journey to Outstanding

Congratulations on picking up this book. It is probably not the first time you are investing into yourself and by doing so, you're clearly setting yourself apart from the majority of people. You're likely among the extraordinary few who don't just dream of a better life—you take action to create one.

Most people stay trapped in a cycle of complaint and frustration, watching their dreams fade while they remain on the sidelines. But you're different - and by opening these pages, you're making powerful declarations. It could be something along the lines of "I am producing results. I am in control of my life, and my standard is outstanding."

Within these pages, you'll discover 72 fundamental and timeless principles that have transformed the lives of countless professionals, entrepreneurs, and leaders. These aren't just theories—they're battle-tested strategies that work.

Ready to accelerate your journey?

Visit www.bright-minds.io to explore our *Success Habits Program*, our community, accountability system and results coaching which can help you create lasting transformation.

SUCCESS FUNDAMENTALS

There is plenty of in-depth material available today in the different disciplines of personal and professional development. However, for most people, success falters at the basics—principles they either aren't aware of or don't consistently implement.

Fundamentals are defined as the simplest, most important elements, ideas, or principles of something—in contrast to more complex concepts. This book focuses on the fundamentals of success and fulfillment, broken down into 72 memorable principles structured into 5 phases.

These principles, with their related theories and practices, have not just been applied by myself and my clients. Consider that these are universal principles—patterns of success and fulfillment that have existed for thousands of years. They have been applied by thousands or millions of the most successful people throughout human history. I learned most of these fundamentals from my mentors and trainers—some of the greatest minds in psychology, tech, and personal development.

Although these principles have existed for hundreds and thousands of years, with each generation of teachers and trainers, they have been developed further. The value this book brings to you is that it delivers the most relevant fundamentals for tech professionals, executives, and entrepreneurs—structured, with a best-in-class learning experience, and ways to help you consistently apply them.

At the end of the book, you'll find the link to a 10-day challenge—read thoughtfully to prepare yourself for it. You'll also discover ways to continue with Bright Minds through our coaching programs, 1:1 coaching, and our community and system. Whether you choose to continue with us or not, this book will provide immense value. Mastering even a few of these fundamentals consistently will unlock your next level of achievement.

That's my promise to you. Let's begin.

PREFACE

About the Author

Tilman Resch's journey began in a small town and led him to become a transformative leader in the tech industry and personal development space. As a certified NLP Coach, Trainer, MBA holder, and M.Sc. Engineer, he brings a unique blend of technical expertise and deep human understanding to his work. At Amazon Web Services (AWS), he has led transformation and customer teams in fast-paced environments, consistently driving results and empowering team members to excel. Having closed 9-digit deals and leading successful teams at one of the world's most innovative companies, Tilman knows firsthand what it takes to achieve exceptional professional results while maintaining personal wellbeing.

But his journey wasn't always smooth. Growing up with self-doubt and limiting beliefs, Tilman discovered that true success requires more than just technical skills or business acumen. Managing side businesses for almost a decade alongside his demanding tech roles taught him crucial lessons about time management. These realizations led him to dive deeper into mindset, success factor modeling, and personal development, learning from world-class mentors including Richard Bandler, John Grinder, Robert Dilts, and Tony Robbins. Through this journey, he not only transformed his own life—multiplying his income several times over—but also discovered his passion for helping others reach their full potential.

Through Bright Minds coaching and the *Success Habits Program*, Tilman has helped hundreds of professionals, entrepreneurs, and executives break through their inner obstacles to achieve significant outcomes. His approach combines proven success principles with practical, executable strategies that work in today's fast-paced world. Whether leading corporate training sessions with MindsetMaps International or working one-on-one with clients, Tilman's mission remains constant: helping people achieve extraordinary professional success while maintaining balance, fulfillment, and joy in their lives.

Tilman continues his own growth journey, practicing the very principles he teaches. His unique value lies not in presenting abstract theories, but in delivering battle-tested strategies that have worked for both himself and his clients. This book distills the essence of what he's learned about creating lasting success—without sacrificing mental health or personal happiness in the process.

Define your Personal Why for Reading this Book

Before diving into our 5-Phase system and 72 Fundamentals, I encourage you to define your personal "why" for reading this book. There are three important reasons for this.

First, by giving meaning to our actions, we multiply both our impact and our fulfillment in the process. Would you like to do both—make the most of this book and enjoy reading it as much as possible?

The second reason relates to defining the direction of your transformation. Tony Robbins captures this with two powerful quotes: "Where focus goes, energy flows" and "The quality of your life depends on the quality of the questions you ask yourself." It's crucial to define your "why" in terms of moving toward something you want, rather than away from something you don't want. When moving toward something, you have a clear direction and destination. When moving away from something, you could potentially go anywhere—just out of that uncomfortable or dangerous situation.

The third reason is that defining your "why" and being emotionally invested in it will help you remember more of the book and increase the likelihood of implementing what you learn. For a deep dive into this effect, I recommend the book "Limitless" by brain coach and entrepreneur Jim Kwik. He explains how to maximize the impact of our learning in the context of reading and personal/professional development. The key takeaway relevant here is: When you approach something with clear intention and purpose, it creates exponentially greater learning benefits and directed progress.

Take a moment to write down why you're reading this book and what success truly means to you. Don't worry about perfection —we'll dive deeper into many of these topics later in the book so that you can refine your answers. But make sure you do the exercise, as this will influence how you engage with every principle and practice that follows.

Find a quiet space and thoughtfully answer these five questions. Feel free to share them with us via info@bright-minds.io:

1. What are the three goals you want to achieve in the next 3 months?
2. What are the three biggest changes you want to make in your life in the next 3 years?
3. What deserves more space in your life, now and in the future?
4. What might be holding you back from reaching your next level?
5. If all the knowledge, skills, and resources were available to you, what would be your ultimate edge?

Common Motivations of Bright Minds Clients

After you've defined your personal "why," let me share some additional inspiration about what clients typically achieve with Bright Minds. And before I list specific outcomes, let me say this: while this learning journey can bring you significant measurable results, it's about so much more. These principles can fundamentally transform the way you see the world, improve your relationships, and create lasting positive change in every area of your life.

Typically, our clients come to us seeking three key outcomes: to increase their results (often financial), to improve their time management and effectiveness, and to master their mindset. This last goal includes overcoming inner obstacles and negative emotions like stress, while developing a success-oriented mindset. Here are the three main outcomes that Bright Minds can help you achieve:

1. **A breakthrough in your career:** Master your mindset for more recognition, higher salary, a promotion, or a new position or dream job. It could also mean taking a step you've wanted to take for a long time, like creating your own business. Or simply becoming a better leader to your teams.
2. **Making more time for what you love:** This could mean finding 2-4 hours each day to do what truly matters to you—like building a successful side business, learning a skill, following a hobby, or spending real quality time with people you love.
3. **Fulfillment and mental health along the process:** Gain the certainty that you can proactively control your emotions, beliefs, and identity; develop clarity about what you want, as well as the discipline and effective systems to follow through.

I've witnessed it countless times—how even a single concept or coaching session can create deep and lasting transformative impacts. These shifts can transform not only your professional career but also your entire life, affecting any personal goal you set for yourself. Think of physical results like weight loss and increased daily vitality. Or—to return to the name of our signature program Success Habits—establishing powerful new routines that serve you every day.

Notes of Gratitude

I extend my deepest gratitude to my mentors, trainers, and anyone I consider part of my team. You have shaped my path and inspired many of the principles of this book.

To **Tony Robbins**, who makes complex concepts accessible to millions. Tony inspired me not just through his seminars, books, and coaching system—but also by demonstrating what it means to "play full out" when serving your audience. He often runs his seminars until deep in the night, ensuring each participant receives maximum value.

To **Robert Dilts**, one of the major influencers of Neuro-Linguistic Programming. Robert has spent decades studying the world's top leaders and entrepreneurs, making their patterns accessible to learn and replicate through success factor modeling. He has coached visionaries like Steve Jobs and led Silicon Valley entrepreneur Masterminds. Two key takeaways from being coached by Robert: I learned coaching mastery at another level of depth, and I understood how personal/professional development and the tech/startup industry are deeply interconnected.

To **Mickey A. Feher**, author and CEO of MindsetMaps International, the world's leading mindset assessment test. Thank you for your mentorship, certifying me as an advanced MindsetMaps coach—and providing such clarity on the different levels and facets of mindset transformation and conscious leadership.

To **John Grinder**, co-founder of NLP, who guided me toward a deeper connection with my unconscious mind and intuition in coaching. And to NLP co-founder Richard Bandler, who taught me the power of direct truth in facilitating meaningful change.

To **Jeff Bezos**, founder and ex-CEO of Amazon. Jeff's journey building Amazon into what it has become today, starting from a vision in the early '90s, is remarkable. I continue learning invaluable lessons on leadership, corporate culture, and true customer focus each day at Amazon Web Services.

To **Blair Singer**, one of the world's best on-stage trainers and facilitators. Blair taught me to facilitate large group training and the crucial importance of context in any training, business, or personal interaction. He also taught me essential persuasion skills, which are vital to fulfilling my mission with Bright Minds.

To **Mac Attram**, one of the leading business coaches based in the UK. Mac helped me transform Bright Minds from a solopreneurship into a business capable of reaching and helping more people. Thank you also for the lessons in sales, coaching, and creating an empowering context in which entrepreneurs can inspire themselves.

To **Tim Grover**, coach of sports legends such as former NBA champion Michael Jordan and author of 'Relentless'. Thank you for validating many of the choices I made to pursue my mission. Relentlessness is a natural instinct within us—allowing it can bring deep fulfillment and joy.

To my coach **Daniel Montes de Oca**, one of Tony Robbins' top coaches—thank you for consistently helping me break through inner obstacles and raising my standards. Thank you for being one of the most high-energy people I know.

To my early Amazon Web Services mentors including **Joerg**

Deibert and **Florian Garlet**; and to **Jochen Walter**, Head of Software Business Germany, who entrusted me early in my career with three of our top five software clients and the responsibility of leading global teams. I am also grateful for the AWS culture, which supported me in building some of the most significant tech partnerships in Europe with global impact while consistently allowing me to follow my passions inside and outside the organization.

To those who saw potential in me early on and pre-credited me with trust—much more than I would have credited myself back then. These people include my school politics teacher **Werner Schwinn**, and especially **Knut Stannowski**, CEO of Collège des Ingénieurs. Your belief made a difference and gave me an identity shift as well.

To my executive assistant **Julia Grzelak**, who is a master when it comes to the power of manifestations in all forms, a singer and songwriter, and generally speaking one of the most beautiful souls I know. Thank you for helping me keep the energy high, asking the right questions when needed—and being one of the driving forces of Bright Minds.

To my grandfather, **Josef Hoffmann**, a leader to both his family and community, to whom I dedicate a special tribute at the end of this book.

To all other mentors and partners who have inspired and supported me along the way, including my joint venture partner **Gabby Attar** (Executive Coach and NLP Trainer) and my writing mentor **Javier Riviero-Díaz** (Author and Entrepreneur). Also to **Marion Hödl** and **Simon Matthias**, who teach at NLP-Center Berlin, my first coaches and trainers—who have had a deep impact on me.

To my family and closest friends.

INTRODUCTION

I sincerely believe that things in life happen for a reason - I believe in the existence of Grace, and that life happens for us, not to us. In that sense, also you have picked up this book for a reason. I am pretty certain that you have already achieved outstanding things in life. And sometimes, we just do not sufficiently recognize that. At the same time, <u>you know</u> that there is another level, in both your private and professional life. This is where it all starts.

The Starting Point

At the beginning of any transformation lies the recognition that there's a gap between where you are and where you want to be. This gap is completely natural, and we could positively rephrase it as "space for growth." If we do not recognize this space, then transformation cannot happen. So as a starting point, let's be truthful about where we are and where we want to go. Along the journey, there will inevitably be obstacles—which we can again rephrase positively as "opportunities for learning, growth and breakthrough."

This has been true for me personally as well: after defining what I wanted and being truthful about the spaces for growth, I encountered obstacles along the way—which led me to create my own success habits. Those habits and insights, enriched with over a decade of experience, trial and error, and coaching, then became the foundation of my coaching program with the same name. So all of this was created out of necessity, to run a business on the side and lead a fulfilled private life, alongside my ambitions in my corporate career.

Each challenge brings its unique demands, but also unique opportunities to learn and grow. Any challenges that you encounter from here on—in this book, or in other contexts—try to approach them with a similar mindset.

Progress and Patterns of Success

The most natural way that learning happens in nature is through trial and error. We set a goal, take action, and if our approach doesn't work, we adapt and try again. Most adults, however, do not even get to that point—they don't even try. The second most common reason people fall short is giving up after their first attempt—never discovering what might have worked on the second or third try.

Trial and error is crucial, and ideally more than once, as highlighted. But how can you accelerate your progress beyond that? When we reflect on this, it becomes crystal clear: capturing learnings after each attempt and building on what works—instead of starting from scratch every time—by using patterns of success. This is exactly the core idea of this book, and this is why coaching and personal development exist. "Success leaves clues," as Tony Robbins often says. There's a reason why certain people consistently create successful outcomes, regardless of external challenges. They follow specific patterns—repeatable behaviors that amplify and accelerate their results. Are you ready to learn those patterns of success?

Execution is Key: Act Upon the Patterns of Success

You'll discover distinct success patterns throughout these pages. Your conscious and subconscious mind will absorb many of them. However, we live in an age of unprecedented distraction—where not only countless people but also trillion-dollar businesses compete for your time and attention on their platforms.

We have to be more focused than ever—and be truly conscious

about taking proactive action toward what we want. This is why we're putting an explicit emphasis on execution throughout this book. I encourage you to not only read through the chapters but also do the exercises and really embody the 72 Fundamentals. This book is not just a collection of theory—it is also a way for you to set even higher standards for yourself, recalibrate your mindset, and take action based on what you actually want— your vision and purpose.

Why SUCCESS FUNDAMENTALS

As defined earlier, fundamentals are "basics" and as the term implies, they are doable. This means anyone can implement these practices of mindset and behavior—it is mainly a matter of motivation and discipline to do so.

The term "fundamental" also means that something is grounded and connected. Think about it—when we experience mental wealth, fulfillment, and success, we can be deeply connected with ourselves and with anyone or anything around us: including people, nature, and the Universe. And that feeling can truly ground us. Fundamentals are something evolutionary, something natural, something grounding—and something crucially necessary. But just as much as they have a minimalistic and modest sense, these fundamental principles can boost your professional, business, and life outcomes to the next level.

The opposite of simplicity is complexity—and in the 21st century era, with unlimited possibilities, the complexity can be overwhelming when we do not manage our lives consciously. Often, my clients don't know where to start, so in the first coaching session, we often spend 10-30 minutes just focusing on the outcome. In today's world, clarity becomes crucial, more than anything else: clarity about what to achieve, why to achieve it, and how to do it. When you apply the **72 Success Fundamentals** from this book, you'll bring your clarity to a whole new level. From that clarity, directed focus and action, breakthroughs and success will naturally follow.

The SUCCESS HABITS model by Bright Minds

This book is structured based on the SUCCESS HABITS model from Bright Minds—it consists of 5 Phases that reflect my personal growth path as well. I structured and started creating the model during several morning routines in a state of ultimate focus and clarity in August 2023, right after an Unleash The Power Within event by Tony Robbins in Birmingham.

The sequence follows a natural progression. While we could start anywhere with personal and professional development—this particular sequence makes sense because one phase builds on top of the next one. Once these patterns and principles become muscle memory, you'll apply them intuitively. Here are the 5 Phases:

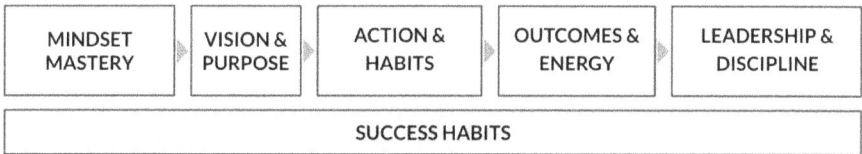

MINDSET MASTERY	VISION & PURPOSE	ACTION & HABITS	OUTCOMES & ENERGY	LEADERSHIP & DISCIPLINE

SUCCESS HABITS

1. **MINDSET MASTERY:** Master the psychology of success and learn to transform limiting beliefs into empowering ones. Develop emotional intelligence and communication skills that set you apart.
2. **VISION & PURPOSE:** Define your compelling future and create alignment between your career goals and personal fulfillment. Craft a clear mission that drives sustainable motivation.
3. **ACTION & HABITS:** Build powerful daily routines and prioritization systems that maximize your impact. Learn to make time for what truly matters while achieving more.
4. **OUTCOMES & ENERGY:** Master deep work, outcome-based organization, and energy management across all

dimensions - body, mind, heart, and spirit. Create sustainable high performance.

5. **LEADERSHIP & DISCIPLINE:** Develop unwavering self-discipline and accountability. Learn to lead yourself and others effectively while maintaining work-life harmony. Create an environment to strive.

Participants in the SUCCESS HABITS Program explore these phases in depth through a comprehensive system of exercises, video training, coaching sessions, mastermind groups, and a supportive community over 3-6 months. Our Bright Minds app provides an accountability system and helps the participants to stay consistent in their implementation. I sincerely encourage you to consider joining the program because it contains the best from Personal Development and its positive effects can be life-changing. You can find more information on our website www.bright-minds.io

Why Do We Start with Mindset?

When you consider your most important goals for the next 3-36 months, you likely think first of external, measurable outcomes: such as a significant salary increase, landing a new job, boosting productivity by 50%, doubling business revenue, or reducing your work week by 8-10 hours while maintaining or improving results.

But what is the driving force that really determines whether you achieve these outcomes? At least when it comes to the things that you can influence—which is much more than we often think? It's our behavior—how we show up each day, the decisions we make, and the actions we take. And these behaviors, along with our emotional states and ultimate potential, all stem from invisible forces within us: our **mindset**. This internal foundation is where everything begins. When we become conscious of our mindset's power and actively develop it, we unlock the ultimate source of both achievement and fulfillment.

> *"If you want to make minor changes in your life, work on your behavior. But if you want to make significant, quantum breakthroughs, work on your mindset [paradigms]."*
>
> —Stephen R. Covey

The model on the next page, developed by my mentors Robert Dilts and Mickey Feher, illustrates how mindset serves as the fundamental driver of successful outcomes.

Cause and Effect

OUTCOMES AND RESULTS

Key Performance Indicators
Signposts to Success

Behaviors

MINDSET

EFFECT

CAUSE

QUANTITATIVE

QUALITATIVE

A NEW MODEL OF THE WORLD

Before we dive into the 5 Phases including our **72 Success Fundamentals** and to set the appropriate context, let me share some theories that may expand your perspective on the world—just as they did for me when I first encountered them.

Personal Growth and Development
Increases Success Exponentially

Training and development of our professional skills is important. There are skills that we learn at university (theories, problem-solving skills) or practical skills about business management, accounting, or sales. Learning such theoretical skills is and will increasingly be important in the professional world. "The market does not sleep" as my mentor Mac Attram likes to say. We need to continuously educate ourselves in our field, whether it's technology, medicine, social science, or law. And we need to apply what we have learned, and we have to stay up to date. These professional skills, however, have somewhat become a hygiene factor or expected requirement in today's world. They are important, but we are competing with many others in the market—so growth may take time if we "only" take this necessary conventional approach. Global markets are becoming increasingly competitive, not even to mention AI.

How do we really set ourselves apart? I am sure there are many achievers reading this book, so you probably already have a unique positioning. But still, how can you get beyond that—and grow so that you really make sure you're playing in the "first league"? This is where it is necessary to add Personal Development into the equation—this means to work with our mindset. When you work on your own operating system, this is when you raise the bar for any moment and outcome in your life, and this is when you can expect exponential breakthroughs and yields. I encourage you, if you are not already doing it, to put even more energy and focus into developing yourself. To me personally, this has unlocked so much in my life—and not just financial wealth, but also emotional wealth. And it has led me to meet even more unique and inspiring personalities, including entrepreneurs. The below graphic, which I learned from my mentor Blair Singer, illustrates how Personal Development can boost our outcomes and success.

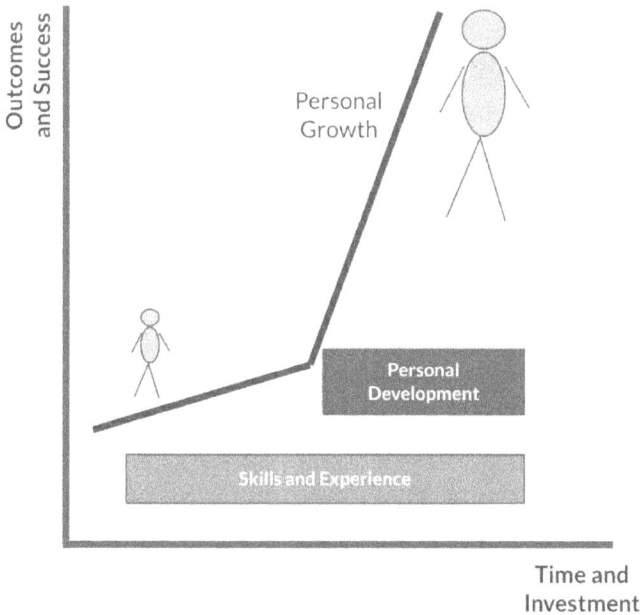

Why must we continuously grow, and cannot stay stagnant? The explanation goes back to core principles of nature. Anything in nature either grows or dies, as Tony Robbins says. There must be movement and progress, for life and for meaning. As you are reading this book, you are probably already on one or another path of personal evolvement and growth, and open to accelerate it. Be grateful about this level of consciousness and insight, and the power that you have to live life on your terms. Once you learn certain tool sets, and truly embark on that journey of constant growth—you can virtually overcome any obstacle and create the life that you want.

A New Model of Reality. Do you Choose the Red Pill?

Have you watched the movie Matrix, where Neo, the chosen one, can choose between the blue pill and the red pill? The blue pill represents reality as we know it—an analogy for the rules, values, and beliefs that society has taught us. The red pill represents a new reality: a deeper truth that may change everything once you grasp it. It can even make you question certain things you believed to be true about the world. It may take you out of your comfort zone and encourage you to make different decisions. To give a personal example: with my "red-pill" evoked mindset, my comfort zone is getting up at 4:30 in the morning, being joyous and enthusiastic about it because of what I can create in those early hours.

Note that if you choose the red pill, it may make you question certain habits you've been used to, things you've always done in particular ways. It may make you question assumptions about the world, people, and the environment. And it may make you reflect on some deeply ingrained values, beliefs, and even your identity in new and different ways.

The potential rewards, however, are significant. Out of temporary discomfort, things will start sorting out in new ways. And you will develop a sense of certainty that can transform your mindset and model of the world, allowing you to live life on your own terms—maximizing both your personal fulfillment and the contribution you can make to others.

Are you ready to taste the red pill?

I personally experienced how powerful the red pill is—not only for my measurable outcomes but also for my relationships and how I live and enjoy each moment. Once I became aware of it, just like in the Matrix movie, I realized how relatively few people are really aware of the red pill: which is an analogy for designing life by your own standards, based on your own purpose and vision, with a model of yourself and the world that truly serves you.

I have made it my mission to educate people about these principles and help them change their lives—sometimes through a whole set of habits, but sometimes through just marginal shifts that can transform anything from great to outstanding. These shifts help people make better choices, create new meanings, and achieve greater results—and this is what Bright Minds helps them with.

"My mission is to inspire, educate and empower people to live a long and truly fulfilled life which they desire, become their best selves, and make their greatest contributions. (...)"

— Personal Mission Statement by Tilman Resch

Basic Principles for a New Model of the World

The following principles are important foundations for many of the things you will learn throughout this book. If you are interested in diving deeper into these and additional theories, you can research NLP (Neuro-Linguistic Programming) Presuppositions.

Proactivity: We have the freedom to choose at every moment. Our feelings, actions, and even our unconscious patterns are within our control. From our sense of belonging and identity to our values, beliefs, internal strategies, skills, actions, and the environment we create—we can be proactive about all of it. As long as we maintain the right state of mind, we always have choices available to us.

Constructivism: Each person has their own unique map of the world. We all act based on our internal map of reality, which is neither objective truth nor identical to anyone else's perspective. This means we can choose to adopt new models of reality. Instead of questioning new concepts—whether it's meditation, energy exchange between humans, or unconscious communication—ask yourself: "How could this insight benefit me?"

Cybernetics: This is the study of how systems control and regulate themselves. The key insight is that changing one part of a system can trigger powerful changes throughout. Consider a challenging relationship: any shift in the system—whether adding another person or changing your own behavior or attitude—can transform the entire dynamic.

Learning and Change: There is no failure, only learning and feedback. When one approach doesn't work, try something different. Thomas Edison had 2,774 learning experiences before creating a functioning electric light bulb. (I've eliminated the word "failure" from my vocabulary and this book.) Every experience becomes valuable when you focus on learning from it.

Communication: We are always communicating, whether we intend to or not. It's impossible not to communicate. The effectiveness of your communication is measured by the response you receive.

Exercise: Reflect on These Five Principles

1. *Take a moment to consider each principle:*
   - *Which principles resonate with your existing worldview?*
   - *Which ones feel new or challenge your current thinking?*
   - *How have you seen these principles at work in your own life?*
2. *Expanding Your Model of the World:*
   - *What beliefs or assumptions might be limiting your current perspective?*
   - *Which of these principles, if fully embraced, would most impact your life?*
   - *What specific actions could you take to integrate these principles into your daily thinking and behavior?*

THE SUCCESS HABITS
5-STEP MODEL

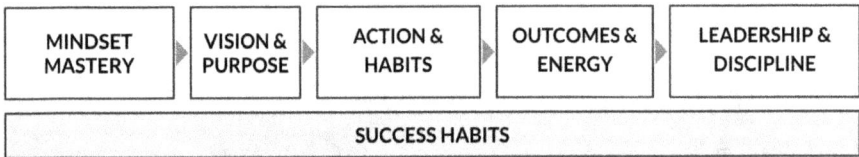

MINDSET MASTERY	VISION & PURPOSE	ACTION & HABITS	OUTCOMES & ENERGY	LEADERSHIP & DISCIPLINE

SUCCESS HABITS

PHASE 1: MINDSET MASTERY

Our mindset forms the foundation of our success and emotional well-being, as highlighted in the introduction. This first chapter has two key objectives:

1. Provide you with deeper **understanding** and **clarity** about your mindset: its origins, how it shapes your perception of the world, and how it determines your reality.
2. Equip you with the insight, confidence, and concrete tools to strengthen or transform your mindset in ways that serve you.

1.1 Focus on the Positive

Let's begin by acknowledging what's already great in your life. I advocate for starting everything with a positive focus—whether it's a business meeting, a conversation, daily reflection, or a coaching session. A positive mental frame puts us in a more resourceful state, increasing our energy and clarity. In this state, we have greater capacity to create, innovate, and prosper. The alternative—focusing on what's missing, lacking, or what we're not good at—can trigger a negative spiral of self-blame, regret, unworthiness, and fight-or-flight responses. As Tony Robbins says: "You become what you focus on." So what do you choose to focus on?

Consider the law of attraction, which is another great representation of that concept: Focusing on positive emotions attracts more positive emotions. Focusing on success brings more success. Sincerely smiling at another person will typically get you a smile in return. Loving yourself will enable you to give more love, and others to share more love with you in return. While the law of attraction is part of many personal development books, I particularly recommend "The Gap and the Gain" by Dan Sullivan for a deeper dive into the power of positive focus. According to Dan, to practice a more positive focus in your everyday life, include the following into your daily rituals: First, connect with three things you are grateful for in your morning routine or meditation. Second, write down three gains or wins of the day in your journal during your evening routine.

How Your Own State Affects Others

Your focus determines your state, which others interpret both consciously and subconsciously. Remember that your focus—

positive or negative—impacts not just you but everyone around you. As a leader, how you show up directly influences your team's mood. Set high standards and be proactive. If you tolerate people in your professional or private life who consistently lower energy levels with negativity, it's your responsibility to address it.

Fundamental 1: Focus on the positive and make this your default mental state. This will create both personal resourcefulness and ripple effects that elevate others.

This first principle, though simple, can significantly enhance your quality of life. Throughout this book, you'll discover numerous ways to create and maintain a positive focus.

1.2 Connecting with your Results, Strengths and What You Love

In line with the positive focus, let us become more concrete and explore several aspects of your greatness. The following exercise will help you connect with your extraordinary results, your power and your passion. When you do it, make sure to take a few minutes of your time, relax and ideally write down the answers in your journal. I recommend writing with your hands whenever possible. Personally, I use an iPad and the Goodnotes application to collect and structure all my notes.

Exercise: Write down...
  1. *Results or things that you are proud of.*
  2. *Special skills that you have.*
  3. *Passions and activities that you love doing.*

The Power of Connecting with Your Resources

Look at the things you have written down and truly connect with them. Stand like you were standing in these moments of victory, fully connected with your strengths. Concentrate fully on these powerful moments and pay attention to the inner dialogue that this creates.

Can you sense how your state changes from doing this exercise? Typically, this will affect the way you stand, move and breathe (physiology), the way you feel (emotions) and your beliefs or what you say to yourself (inner language). We will explain the concept of state and how you can anchor a positive state in depth in an upcoming chapter.

For the sake of this exercise: make clear to yourself that

these are resources inside of you and that you can re-activate them whenever they may serve you. All you need to do is to consciously connect with them. Also note that many of the goals that you have written down probably seemed far away or hard to achieve at some point in your life. Or even unachievable? But you have figured out ways and mastered it, you have achieved those results that once were a dream or vision. We have the ability to master and reach so much more than we think we are capable of.

Fundamental 2: Know what your strengths and superpowers are—connect with them every day, and continuously develop them.

The Deeper Meaning Behind Your Passions

Passions are activities that you feel truly immersed in and in flow with—you simply love them. When you practice your passions, they create high levels of energy rather than consuming it. Now look again at the passions you wrote down. Where do they originate from? One area to explore is the question of what is the greater meaning behind passion. Another is the realization that your passions have a history, they originate from somewhere. At some point in your life, something gave you a sense or meaning to really focus on that area—which now fills you with positive emotions. That understanding, along with the insight that feeling passionate about something is a state, brings us to the conclusion that passions are something we can be proactive about.

Say you are passionate about one activity and you know your state when you are experiencing this. You would like to be passionate about another activity as well, because you know that it is important for you and would be aligned with your purpose or mission in life—for example being passionate about working out, coaching your team, doing that morning routine, or playing with your child. To increase your level of passion about an activity, there are three best practices: First, find a common meaning with something that you are already passionate about. Second, attach a similar set of emotions to it, as to one of your passions. Third, practice it regularly—make it a habit so that it becomes really seamless to you. If this seems still abstract to you—you will get a better understanding of it in this book, or you can approach it in a Bright Minds advanced program or 1:1 coaching.

"Hard times will come. And passion is what makes the difference: the passionate people go on. The rational ones just give up."
- Steve Jobs

Fundamental 3: Passion fuels energy. Nurture existing passions and intentionally cultivate new ones in life areas you want to embrace fully.

1.3 Unconditional Emotions

What does success mean for you? Often, we associate success with specific outcomes or possessions. Professionally, this might mean getting promoted, acquiring a certain job title, gaining more responsibility, increasing salary, winning new clients, growing revenue, becoming a market leader, or achieving financial freedom. In our personal lives, it might mean specific goals in someone's relationship or family, owning a particular house, buying a special watch, having the flexibility to take three days off weekly, or something as simple but important as being a great partner.

Breaking Free from Conditional Emotions

The true reason we desire these outcomes lies in the emotions we expect to feel when we achieve them—feelings of freedom, pride, power, love, connection, balance, joy, calmness, accomplishment, and gratitude. For instance, one of my clients pursued a Director position, associating it with feelings of achievement, self-recognition, and greater calmness. Now there's nothing against striving for that position. But why procrastinate these wonderful emotions? That is the first common pitfall - to make positive emotions conditional - instead of just inviting them. Without a particular reason, or we could relate them to something we have already achieved.

The next issue is, and this relates to the previous one as well, that we allow and experience the emotions that come along with the success, often only temporarily. Oftentimes, after accomplishing one goal, high achievers immediately set their sights on the next one. While continuous growth through goal-setting is valuable, the risk is again to deprive oneself from these positive emotions - by making them conditional, and not celebrating wins.

You've likely achieved many outcomes that once seemed like unrealistic dreams. And if you think about it, you can probably recall several or many moments of accomplishment in which you experienced emotions of success, pride, and victory. You've also likely experienced moments of tremendous love, joy, or playfulness.

So most of us are very familiar with those feelings, at least temporarily - and by the way, if this is not the case for you, I would recommend bringing this up in a coaching session. Since we are familiar with those feelings, here's the powerful twist: instead of waiting for outcomes to experience these emotions, allow yourself to feel them regularly. You can incorporate them into your gratitude or meditation practice, celebrate small wins throughout the day, or exchange a smile and feelings of connection with others. As these emotions become more familiar, you'll access them more easily and frequently. Personally, I embody and anchor positive emotions through affirmations, first thing in the morning during my routine.

Fundamental 4: Success emotions are a choice, not a destination. Access and experience positive emotions daily, rather than making them conditional on future achievements.

1.4 Our Emotional Home and How to Create an Inner Palace

The Origins of Our Emotional Patterns

We humans are habitual creatures, and many of these habits throughout human history have been crucial for survival. Tens of thousands of years ago, it made sense to be scared and stressed often to avoid being killed or eaten by dangerous animals. If we look, for example, at the emotion of fear: from an evolutionary standpoint, for the longest time of our human existence, and needless to explain, the negative emotion of fear has been crucial for our survival.

How Emotional Patterns Form in Childhood

In a sense, they still are today in certain moments. Let's look at small babies, who depend on their parents so much that not being loved and nurtured could mean death. So instinctively, babies cry to get their parents' attention and care, as it is crucial for survival. We can also say that the act of crying is a so-called coping strategy of the baby to get nutrition and love, caused by the unconscious emotion of fear of death. Let's look at a second example regarding coping strategies - a 5-year-old may not feel seen and loved by their parents, as they give them little attention. The kid may now try to impress their parents in different ways - in order to be seen and loved, which is subconsciously still rooted in the attempt to receive love and nurturing as these are crucial for survival.

Breaking Free from Negative Neural Circuits

In an ideal world, in peaceful environments, these neural

circuits would be less activated in childhood - and at least overwritten until adulthood. In reality though, this is not always the case and even the opposite happens: negative emotional patterns can be deeply rooted and anchored in someone's mind. What happens is this: as these neural circuits are somewhat familiar, they get fired over and over again, so that these negative emotions only get re-emphasized. As Tony Robbins says, "what fires together wires together."

These neural circuits, when triggered again and again, can become so familiar to a person that they are basically addicted to them - and tend to fall back into them over and over again. It may be ugly, but at least it is familiar. This is a negative example of how an emotional home can be created - and why so many people, especially in our Western world, live primarily in negative emotional states; and normal education does not teach us to "unwire" them and be proactive about changing them.

EMOTIONAL
HOME

Clarity   Pride
        Love
              Calmness
Joy
     Accomplishment

Happiness   Fear

Motivation   Anger
   Gratitude   Resentment

44

Creating a Positive Emotional Home

As highlighted earlier: in life, we get what we focus on. To maximize your success and fulfillment, it is therefore important that you declutter your emotional home and ensure that your default state is a positive one. Again, since the law of attraction will make you attract more positive anything into your life. Besides that, well - life just feels so much better that way.

Developing a Sensitiveness About Something Being Off

There is another practical reason why a primarily positive state is so powerful - and of course I know this very well from my own experience too. As my default state is positive, then whenever I feel a negative emotion more consistently or for no reason, then it is a sign that something might be off track. So any negative emotion is like a messenger. It is how my intuition, my subconscious communicates with me - and something to explore, to be curious about.

As a consequence, I believe that a decluttered emotional home will give much better access to one's intuition. Based on any deviation, we can connect with that emotion: recognize it, feel it, listen to it, be curious about it. Have that sense that there is something behind this emotion that probably seeks to be held, understood or healed - as Robert Dilts would say it. So to summarize: Coming from a healthy and sorted emotional home, any negative emotion can be a powerful signal.

Exercise: Design Your Emotional Palace

Reflect on your emotional patterns and create your own emotional palace through these steps:

1. **Map Your Current Emotions**
   - *On one page of your journal, create two columns: "Positive Emotions" and "Negative Emotions"*
   - *List the emotions you've experienced regularly over the past week*
   - *Make a conscious decision to reduce focus on negative emotions*
   - *Note: If certain emotions need healing, consider self-reflection or coaching*

2. **Connect with Your Desired Outcome**
   - *Think about your main goal or desired outcome*
   - *Write down the emotions you expect to feel when achieving it*
   - *Really feel these emotions as you write them down*

3. **Build Your Emotional Palace**
   - *Draw the outline of a house on a new page*
   - *Inside this palace, write all your positive emotions*
   - *Add the positive emotions from your desired outcome*
   - *Remember: This is your emotional home—you can visit it anytime*

4. **Integration Reflection**
   - *Consider how this emotional awareness can: Make your journey more enjoyable, provide important signals for growth and help you achieve better outcomes*

Fundamental 5: Be the designer of your emotional home. Make it a palace, and consciously choose the emotions that reside there on a daily basis.

Fundamental 6: When a negative emotion enters your emotional palace, see it as a messenger. Connect with the feeling, be grateful for it. Understand its message—which may relate to a next level ahead, something to overcome, or something to be done.

1.5 The Power of State Shift

In each moment, your emotional state determines how you perceive reality. Your state determines how you show up in every situation, whether in business or while you are with friends and family. Wouldn't it be powerful to choose your state more consciously? For example, to show up as an empathetic, certain, and heartful leader who gives confidence to others whenever you choose. Or to show up as that reliable person who is ready to execute and get things done - naturally and intuitively.

The good news is that we can proactively change our state within seconds. And it is even something we can practice. But let us first explain the concept. We could go deeper from an NLP perspective here of course, but rather stick to Tony Robbins' concept - as it explains this in such a simple and practical way.

There are three forces that determine our emotional state: patterns of physiology, focus, and language/meaning. Patterns of **physiology** relate to how we use our physical body - breath, posture, movement, and so on. Patterns of **focus** refer to what we direct our attention to, as whatever we focus on, we feel. Patterns of **language/meaning** determine how we interpret our experiences. Note that the moment we put words to an experience, we shape its meaning.

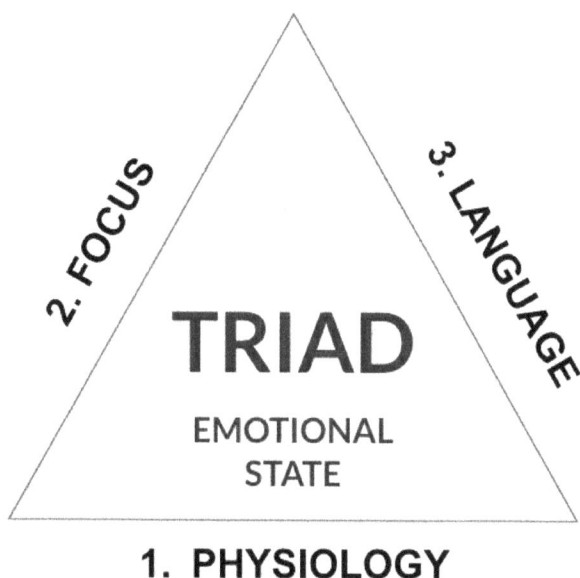

```
        TRIAD
        EMOTIONAL
         STATE
```

2. FOCUS

3. LANGUAGE

1. PHYSIOLOGY

Positive and Negative TRIAD

Think of a person who is feeling depressed. How would he or she stand? Would their head be leaning up or down? Would they focus on positive or negative things or memories? And what beliefs would be present in their minds, what meaning would they give outside events? Now think of a person in a moment of triumph and success. How would they stand, what would they focus on, and what would they believe/ what meanings would they give to the events? The TRIAD of those two persons would be completely different. And as you can imagine, the second person would not only be more creative, powerful and energetic, but also attract more success into their life just like a magnet.

The concept is very straightforward, and here comes another point which makes it so useful: the three elements of the TRIAD are connected. Probably the most simple and oftentimes most powerful state change is to change your physiology. Just changing the way you stand and breathe can change your state entirely. And of course, changing your focus towards what is going well and what you are grateful for, can change your state entirely too. And giving a positive meaning to a situation, can again totally change your state in a positive way as well. The most effective state change happens, if you combine all three forces of the TRIAD.

How to Capture Positive States and Build Powerful Resources

Another beautiful thing about the TRIAD is that you can capture these beautiful states once you've created them. We call that "anchoring". You can anchor a positive state, for example, in the way you stand. Just lifting up your chest, your chin and your smile a few millimeters can have a significant impact. Once anchored, every time you trigger the state, the neurons in your brain will start firing - and a positive focus as well as positive language will be triggered.

Of course, you can use a different element to create the anchor, for example language through an affirmation, or focus by reminding yourself about the goal. Or a combination of these.

The more often you anchor positive states, the stronger this will get. At some point, you'll be able to fire positive emotions instantly, almost at any moment - every time you enter a room. Here's a trick when you create your positive state: stack different positive emotions on top of each other - from moments of joy, pride, love and achievement - whatever you want your state anchor to provide.

Exercise:

1. *Think of a negative situation, and notice what happens with your physiology, focus and inner language/meaning.*
2. *Now think of a super successful and fulfilled moment. Close your eyes and see what you saw, hear what you heard, feel what you felt. How do you stand, how do you breathe, what do you focus on and what language or beliefs are prevailing in your mind? By being conscious in that state, you automatically anchor it with your physiology.*
3. *Draw a triangle into your journal and write down what you experienced, creating your TRIAD of success.*

Fundamental 7: Master your state through the TRIAD: shift your physiology, mental focus, and inner language. Anchor states of gratitude and achievement to instantly access your success state.

1.6 Six Human Needs: What Drives Our Behavior

In anything that we humans do in our lives, we seek certain outcomes - with the ultimate intention to meet our needs. While values and beliefs (we come to those in the next chapter) are learned, human needs are inborn. This makes them very powerful and one of the main drivers of human action. According to a concept by Tony Robbins, all humans have 6 needs. These are four personal needs: Certainty, Variety, Significance, Connection/Love; and two higher needs: Growth and Contribution. Since all human behavior seeks to fulfill one of those needs, every human action or behavior has some kind of positive intent.

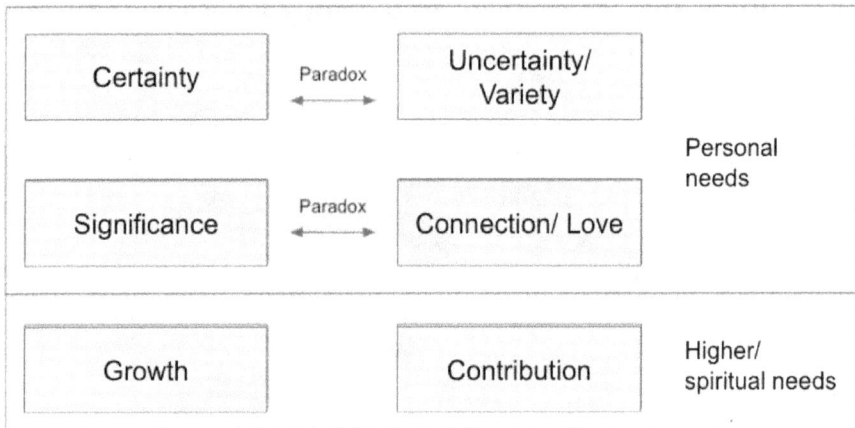

Certainty	Paradox ←→	Uncertainty/ Variety	
Significance	Paradox ←→	Connection/ Love	Personal needs
Growth		Contribution	Higher/ spiritual needs

Let me briefly define what these needs are about:

1. **Certainty:** The strong certainty to experience a certain emotional state, to experience pleasure or to avoid pain.
2. **Variety:** The need to experience variety, seeking the unfamiliar and unknown, change and new stimuli.

3. **Significance:** The feeling of being very unique, important, special or needed by others.
4. **Connection/Love:** The feeling of love and/or connection to someone or something.
5. **Growth:** Learning and evolving, meaning an expansion of understanding and mental capacity. Everything alive must grow; this is a law of nature.
6. **Contribution:** Helping, serving and supporting others, making meaningful contributions.

Prioritizing the Right Needs

While we have all of those needs, there are usually 1-2 ones that we value more than others. The question then arises: what are the vehicles we use to fulfill those needs? Our success, however we define it, is shaped not by our needs so much, but by the way we meet them. And how we meet them is driven by our belief system, map, and rule book.

To give an example: Let's say that three different persons value significance the most. One person feels significant by saving a stranger's life. Another person by taking someone's life. Another person by being ill all the time and communicating about this a lot. They have the same needs structure but different belief systems. This is an extreme example, but it illustrates well that the means we choose to fulfill our needs depends on the underlying belief structure.

So what does that mean for your outcome to be more successful? It is worth reflecting on what needs have been most important for you in the past, are right now - and what needs you will need to prioritize to reach your next level. If your main driver for success has been significance up until now, you want to reconsider, because oftentimes growth and contribution are much more beneficial needs to focus on, for sustainable and fulfilling success.

Fundamental 8: Your needs drive your behavior. Among the 6 Human Needs (Certainty, Uncertainty, Significance, Love/ Connection, Growth, Contribution)—prioritize the ones that best support and align with what matters to you.

1.7 Human Needs: Choosing the Right Vehicles to Fulfill our Needs

The next question is, how do you fulfill those needs? For that, let us look more consciously at the vehicles you use. We start with an example.

In someone's set of habits, there are habits such as overeating after an intense day of work, and smoking one package of cigarettes per day. What kinds of needs do you think smoking could fulfill for that person? Smoking can certainly create a relaxed moment. It brings variety because in the moment of nicotine rush, new perspectives may open up. It may also make someone feel significant - at least that is what advertisements have preached for decades. And someone may even feel a sense of connection with themselves because they consciously take time while doing it.

Now why is smoking such a strong addiction for that person? There are some biochemical effects related to nicotine, but that is just one side of the coin. In fact, another effect is at least as strong: whenever a behavior fulfills 3-4 basic needs, it can become some kind of addiction.

Changing the Vehicle to Fulfill a Need

What could we advise that person to do about it? Obviously, the person needs a new and more healthy vehicle to relax. We would advise the person to do the following:

1. **Identify the most important 1-2 needs**, either in general or in those moments. In this example, this could be (a) certainty to experience a good moment

(since the person has lots of uncertainty in their life), and (b) a moment to connect with themselves or with other smokers (since the person feels lonely). The two major needs here are certainty and love/connection.

2. **Identify a more beneficial behavior/vehicle to fulfill those needs.** A more beneficial way to have certain moments of peace and relaxation, as well as feeling connected with themselves and others, could be doing sports or a Yoga class as group exercise.

   There is a precondition here of course: that the person's model of the world allows them to believe that Yoga or group exercise bring relaxation and connection. If this is not the case, this is something that the person can be proactive about - as long as there's sufficient motivation to change their model of the world. We come to that in later sections of this first chapter.

3. **Practice the New Behavior Habitually** By practicing the new behavior habitually, the person will have regular certainty, self-love and connection in their life. But even more than that, because activities such as meditation, Yoga and workout are multi-dimensional. Such activities not only fulfill the four personal needs but also at least one of the higher needs.

The Power of Your Prevailing Needs

Your needs structure has a strong impact on how you think and behave on a day-to-day basis. Let me give you two examples:

- If you value certainty, you'll most likely know where all the emergency exits are. If you value uncertainty/variety, you're probably convinced that you will get out one way or another, as you always find your way.

- If you value significance, you will want to be unique and

important (which may not be the most sustainable force in many cases). Versus if you create something unique and important from your heart to connect with another person, or want to grow and contribute to the world.

Once you get conscious about your needs and your prevailing vehicles to meet them, you can be proactive about it. Realize where your needs come from, and that you can choose to overwrite them. Realize that we all value either what we got lots of and want more of, or what we were prevented from having, what we felt scarcity of. And seek such vehicles that meet 5-6 of your needs in a strong and positive way: meaning that they meet all 4 personal needs, but in addition your higher/spiritual needs as well.

Exercise:

1. *Ask yourself, which needs do you value most and focus on most in your daily life?*
2. *Would it make sense to refocus on different needs?*
3. *Pick one behavior or habit that you would like to get rid of and replace. What would be a more beneficial vehicle that simultaneously fulfills your higher/spiritual needs?*

Fundamental 9: Consciously choose how you fulfill your Human Needs to create sustainable success and fulfillment. Seek vehicles that serve your growth and contribute to others.

1.8 Bonus Chapter: Human Needs and the Source of Life Fulfillment

Consider a father who feels truly fulfilled in his work because he experiences high levels of certainty, variety, significance, connection, growth, and contribution. Yet this same father might feel unfulfilled when spending time with his children simply because of his perception that these moments don't meet his needs to the same extent. The key insight here is that it's about perception, which can be changed. To transform his perception, he would need to adjust what he notices, what he appreciates, or what he believes.

Living a Fulfilled Life is a Choice

Any activity or vehicle can potentially meet all six needs if we adopt an effective model of the world and an empowering perception or strategy. We can find true fulfillment in virtually any endeavor. The essential questions to ask yourself are: Does this vehicle serve my long-term needs for growth and contribution? Does it help me become a better person? With this realization, life becomes less about whether we can be fulfilled and more about choosing a path to sustainable long-term fulfillment.

As Tony Robbins articulates, our internal driving force stems from our beliefs about how something will affect or fulfill our needs. The crucial distinction is that you possess a set of beliefs, philosophies, and language patterns that determine whether you think someone or something will meet your needs. This forms the driving force behind every thought, feeling, and emotion we experience. By changing these belief patterns, you can meet all six needs through virtually any activity. Once you deeply understand and apply this principle in service of your mission, you discover the secret to finding fulfillment in every moment while growing through everything you do.

Choosing Your Mindset and Vehicles of Fulfillment is Not a One-Way Street

Let me share a personal example to illustrate this concept more practically. As I write this paragraph in November 2024, I've been spending significant time with close friends. During these days, I've experienced profound fulfillment, visible to others through my facial expressions and energy. Through this quality time, I've been able to meet my four personal needs at a high level, while also satisfying my two higher spiritual needs – a conscious choice reflected in how I immerse myself in the moment and connect with others.

Being by myself while fully focusing on my mission and career can give me the highest levels of fulfillment as well (indicated to others through facial expressions and my energy) when I am focusing on my professional mission, which is about leading and driving transformation and change, serving other people, organizations, and the world.

So then it becomes a choice - which activity do I choose and prioritize right now? And then I can balance those out, in whichever way is aligned with my mission and timeline. But you see, the question is not whether I am fulfilled or not. With the right strategy, this is a given. And whenever I feel that something is off - remember that interesting guest in my emotional home - then this is a signal for me to change something, to refocus or to strategize about with my coach.

Choosing Multi-Dimensional Vehicles for Fulfillment

As already mentioned, the secret is to pick those behaviors or activities that meet all of your needs. The first four are your fundamental needs, and these need to be met. But whether you feel truly fulfilled is determined by whether and to what extent you fulfill your two higher/spiritual needs as well. Humans live to grow and to contribute and in fact, this is a universal law of nature: everything alive must grow.

The decisions we take on a day-to-day basis are often primarily determined by our four human needs. Be conscious about it and remember, how you approach the first four will determine whether you'll meet growth and contribution as well.

The Difference Between Achievers and Non-Achievers Most people do not get to such an outstanding and fulfilled life because they find ways to meet their needs, including the two higher ones, at low levels of fulfillment. This happens continuously, until eventually they lose their hunger and as a result, they settle for a mediocre life. They are not very happy, not really unhappy enough to change something. They do not feel on track - never quite sure why they do not feel fulfilled, searching for more answers and for more meaning in life. Or they might not even be searching anymore and just distracting and numbing themselves - away from the pain of the lack of fulfillment. This could be through alcohol, drugs, smoking, watching Netflix - but also through positive vehicles, which they overuse to compensate for the lack of fulfillment. In fact, people numb themselves from the fact that they don't know how to win the game of life.

Your Next Steps Towards Life Fulfillment

At this point, you may think: these are great insights, but what to do next? The answer is of course: apply everything you learn in this book. But to make it very simple: be conscious about your needs and how you fulfill them, as well as the values and beliefs which are strongly influenced by your identity. Align these with your mission and goals, and make sure you put yourself consistently into state.

Note that the insights shared in this bonus chapter go quite deep already - however, I am confident that you get a first sense of it, and my hope is that this enriches your map of the world. While these new distinctions will already make a great difference for you, if you want to go deeper, you can work with a Bright Minds coach. That can be myself, or associate coaches from my team, whom I picked among the best coaches I have met in advanced coaching training. To get to your next level, I encourage you to get coaching at least once per month - personally, I get coached every two weeks.

Fundamental 10: Your perception and strategy for how you perform a certain action determine if and to what extent an activity fulfills your 6 Human Needs. Consciously direct your focus and design a strategy so that the activities that serve your purpose meet all your needs at high levels. You will love those activities.

1.9 Values and Beliefs: Invisible Forces that Determine our Outcomes

Our values and beliefs are part of our subjective perception about ourselves and the world. They play a crucial role in determining which needs we prioritize and how we believe we can best fulfill them. Moreover, through values and beliefs, we give meaning to what happens in our life, making them key factors in every decision we take.

Values and beliefs are not innate - they are shaped throughout our life. As we understand how they are formed, we recognize that values and beliefs, like any other aspect of our mindset, are factors we can proactively influence. We can transform and reprioritize them to become more fulfilled and successful. Let's start with the basic definitions.

Definition: Values

Values are explicit or implicit ideas of what is desirable; they determine how we want to be, what we want to stand for, and how we want to relate to the world around us. Values act as invisible guidelines, influencing what we prioritize in life. We can distinguish between two types of values: Ends are emotional states we pursue (e.g., freedom, love), while Means are the ways to reach those ends (e.g., success, money, influence, family, friendship, loyalty). Values are positive and desirable by definition. The significant difference lies in which values we prioritize most.

Exercise:
> 1. *Write down 10-15 values that are important to you. Circle the ones that matter to you the most.*

2. *Reflect why they matter to you so much.*
3. *Is there something you would change about the prioritization?*

Fundamental 11a: By default, we humans place the highest value on things we once had in abundance, or what we deeply felt the lack of. Choose to be proactive about your values, rather than letting them control you.

Definition: Beliefs

Beliefs are the expression of values. A belief is a feeling of certainty that something has a specific meaning and is the way it is. Beliefs act as invisible rules, often becoming self-fulfilling prophecies that determine outcomes in our life. Helpful beliefs enable us to access our full potential by activating inner resources and abilities to achieve our goals. Conversely, negative or limiting beliefs have the opposite effect, restricting our potential and preventing us from reaching our goals.

Types of beliefs

We can categorize beliefs into three main types. The sum of our beliefs forms our belief system:
1. Beliefs about our identity: "I am..."
2. Beliefs about our capabilities: "I am good at..."
3. Beliefs about the world, including rules: "People are...", "If...then...", "Life is..."

Exercise:
1. *Think about a goal or something that is important to you in life.*
2. *Write down the beliefs that come to mind, looking at those three types of beliefs.*
3. *Briefly reflect and mark the beliefs that serve you, versus*

the ones that do not serve you.

The Origin of Values and Beliefs

Values and beliefs originate from socio-cultural influences and experiences - our country, social groups, religion, company, and the influence of family, friends, and role models. Some of these influences stem from conscious decisions: who we spend time with, where we travel, our educational choices, or what we choose to believe about daily experiences. Other influences were beyond our control, such as our family, hometown, or the culture in which we grew up.

The Mechanism of Value and Belief Conditioning

Beliefs and values are imprinted through strong emotions and/or repetition, with the strongest effects stemming from significant emotional moments or periods in our life. Values become conditioned either when we lack something, creating a gap to be closed, or when we become so accustomed to something that we cannot imagine living without it. Beliefs relate to our values but are more specifically the result of patterns we continuously observe or intensely experience - patterns related to universal truths about ourselves and the world. This imprinting becomes even stronger when we link pain or pleasure to their implications.

Exercise:
1. *Write down three beliefs that limit you or prevent you from reaching your goals.*
2. *Reflect on why you have these beliefs and where you adopted them.*
3. *Write down three beliefs that would serve you and bring you closer to your outcome.*

Fundamental 11b: Our beliefs are conditioned through emotional experiences and repetition. Understand their origins. Just as you created them, you can change them.

1.10 Transforming Limiting Beliefs

Once we have identified limiting beliefs, how do we change them? Realizing it and "telling ourselves the truth" that they exist is an important first step. SOmetimes, we just need to have certain insights and our mind will be relieved and is able to find unlimiting alternatives by itself. In addition, I am providing you here a 3-Step process to transform limiting beliefs.

Note that beliefs are a topic where we can potentially go very deep, and it is something that often comes up in coaching sessions as well. There are many coaching techniques to transform beliefs - so if you have a deeper one that you believe needs a deeper intervention - this is something a coach can very well help you with typically.

Back to what we can influence in this moment - here is the 3-step process. When you apply these steps well, engaging your emotions, they can bring significant transformation:

1. **Find the Positive Intent:** Remember that every part of us has some kind of positive intent. Ask yourself: Is this belief trying to protect you from rejection, pain, or failure? Once you understand the positive intention, you can seek a different, more beneficial belief that serves the same purpose.

2. **Discover Contradicting:** Evidence Find counterexamples that demonstrate when the limiting belief is not true. Look for instances that challenge and contradict your current perspective. This helps create new neural pathways and expands your map of the world.

3. **Create Emotional Leverage:** Reflect on and visualize both the negative consequences this limiting belief has already had on your life and the potential future

consequences if you do not transform it. Link painful consequences to the belief you want to change, and equally link positive consequences to the new belief you want to adopt. Remember: whenever we attach emotion to something, we create a much stronger learning experience.

Your Beliefs Determine Your Results in Life

Why is it so important to work on our belief system? Consider the Cycle of Success shown in the graphic below, which illustrates in a simplified way the impact of beliefs. Your beliefs determine your potential, which influences the actions you take or do not take—which in turn influence your results. When you draw that circle with positive beliefs, it becomes a flywheel —an analogy that we also use at the tech company Amazon. Conversely, with negative beliefs, it becomes a vicious circle, as poor results then re-confirm your limiting beliefs.

Action ⟹ Results

Cycle of
⇧ Success ⇩

Potential ⟸ Belief/
Certainty

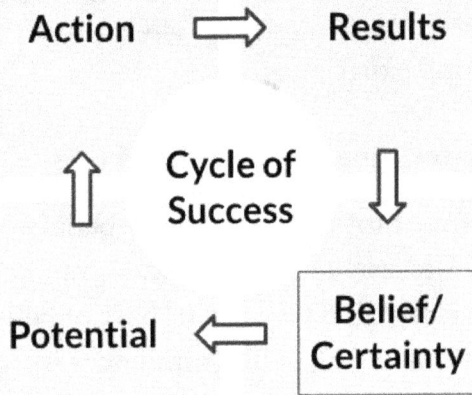

Conditioning New Beliefs

Once you have developed a list of empowering beliefs, make them really stick and maximize their effect by linking them to positive consequences and emotions in both the present and future. The most powerful way to truly embody a new belief or belief system is through the TRIAD. Instead of just speaking out the new belief as an affirmation (language), engage your entire being and truly focus on what you want:

1. **Physical and Emotional engagement:** Stand strong and move your entire body, put a smile on your face or an expression of determination, and truly feel the positive emotions when you speak out these empowering beliefs.
2. **Mental Focus and Visualization:** Imagine or envision the positive outcome, focusing on it consciously with clear intention and purpose.

Fundamental 12: Transform limiting beliefs by understanding their positive intent, finding counterexamples, recognizing their potential impact, and fully embodying new empowering beliefs.

1.11 The Fundamentals of Practical Psychology: Understanding How Human Needs, Beliefs, Values, and Emotions Play Together

When we observe others' behavior, it's tempting to make quick assumptions about their motivations. Yet human behavior stems from complex combinations of different driving forces - some people are primarily driven by feeling significant, others by experiencing love or variety, and still others by pursuing growth and contribution. Most commonly, our actions fulfill multiple needs simultaneously.

To truly understand human behavior, we need to think like practical psychologists. This means moving beyond surface-level judgments to explore the deeper forces that shape both our own actions and those of others. By developing this perspective, you'll gain powerful insights into human nature while building your ability to create positive change - both in yourself and in supporting others.

Let's explore this through a practical example. Consider someone who repeatedly engages in a specific behavior pattern. The more fundamental needs this behavior satisfies, the more likely it is to become deeply ingrained and meaningful to them. To illustrate these dynamics, we'll follow the story of Anna, whose situation demonstrates how different psychological factors interact.

Three Aspects of Practical Psychology

6 HUMAN NEEDS Target	INNER MAP i.e. beliefs	EMOTIONS TRIAD

First, there is a **target** Anna is after in life. There is a set of needs that she's trying to meet, which are most important to her and subconsciously drive all her decision-making—influencing where she's going, what she's doing, and what she likes and dislikes.

Second, whether she meets those needs depends on her **inner map of the world**. This map consists of her beliefs, rules, values, fears, and desires, guiding her on how to meet those needs. However, Anna's map of the world—her belief system—might be outdated and was perhaps never updated. She may have developed certain elements of that map years ago that are now disadvantageous, stopping her from reaching her desired destination.

Third, **emotion** is the factor that affects both her needs and her inner map. People often find a primary emotion where they choose to reside. Some individuals can always find a way to feel frustrated, sad, or angry, or to experience deep emotions of insecurity or inadequacy. Hopefully, Anna is different—someone who can find certainty, confidence, or courage, regardless of circumstances. Or someone who can feel playful at will. Whatever emotional patterns Anna has conditioned into her body ultimately filter her map and her needs.

Understanding Someone's Map of the World and Emotions

This understanding enables us to go beyond simple labeling and develop deeper empathy. Instead of quickly categorizing someone—for instance, saying "she is bipolar because she sometimes gets super happy and then incredibly depressed"— we can take time to understand the person.

For example, you may find that Anna is trying to feel significant and wants to get this feeling with certainty. Her dramatic mood swings might stem from the belief that significance is directly tied to financial success. She thinks that once she achieves that, she can feel truly significant. When challenges arise in business and life, and things aren't working out immediately, she concludes that it will never happen. That might be the source, and consequently, her mood may fluctuate dramatically.

This level of analysis and understanding allows us in coaching to evoke substantial transformations. We want to get to the source and understand what needs a person is after. We want to understand their beliefs and determine whether these are outdated and require a shift. Additionally, we seek to understand the emotions they have become addicted to and how these are trained and represented across all aspects of their experience (TRIAD).

To influence someone, you have to know what already influences them. These three forces are what influence our outcomes in life the most. The best leaders are practical psychologists who understand these dynamics both within themselves and within others. We dive deeper into this in the full SUCCESS HABITS program.

Fundamental 13: To be effective as a leader, think like a practical psychologist. First seek to understand the other person by considering their physiology, mental focus, and internal strategies, as well as their language. Pace first, and then serve them by giving guidance and inspiration.

1.12 Fundamentals of Human Transformation (Part 1): Your Blueprint

Let's face it - you might be doing great, but there's likely one or several areas in your life where you're either unsatisfied with the status quo or simply want more. This is a natural process: whenever we set a goal, we acknowledge a gap between where we are and where we want to be. In other words, your life conditions (LC) don't match your blueprint (BP). Tony Robbins expresses this as the formula for life fulfillment and happiness:

$$LC = BP$$

When our life conditions match our blueprint, we feel happy and fulfilled. Our blueprint encompasses our mindset, core expectations, and vision of how life should be. When there's a mismatch, we feel a sense of gap. Upon recognizing this gap, you have two choices:

1. Change your life conditions - transform what you do, adopt a new standard, and become a bigger version of yourself.
2. Change your blueprint - modify your beliefs about how life should be.

Here are four lessons about this concept that I want to share with you. Take these as food for thought. Personally, these helped me, as well as many of my clients.

1. Your blueprint will have different time components. Your ideal life blueprint now might be different from your blueprint in 10 years from now. Make sure that you do not mix them up or compare yourself to your future blueprint. However, it is crucial that your

current blueprint aligns with your future blueprint - so that you're fulfilled in this moment while laying the foundation for the future.

2. When you consider your current and future blueprint, when you zoom out a little and see the bigger picture, and when you think in terms of outcomes rather than tasks, you may realize that you've been a bit hard on yourself sometimes. This is a common trap for achievers. Make sure that your blueprint relates to the outcome, not on satisfying every task that is thrown at you.

3. It can be that a blueprint is not achievable, for example due to physical or biological limitations. In such instances, you have the choice to change your blueprint - for example by changing underlying beliefs on how to satisfy the underlying need - or even making changes in your need structure and prioritization.

4. In many or most cases, you do have the power to reach your ultimate blueprint. At the end of the day, it's a matter of mindset. So let me encourage you to step up, set a new standard for yourself, and take decisive action.

Fundamental 14: The formula for life fulfillment consists of your life conditions and your blueprint: LC = BP. Remember that you are responsible for your blueprint, and in most cases for your life conditions too.

1.13 Fundamentals of Human Transformation (Part 2): Motivation - The Carrot and Stick

At this point in the book, you may have had some breakthroughs already, or at least gained more clarity about what you want to transform in your mindset and why. There's one more crucial factor critical to trigger effective and lasting transformation: leverage. Let me explain the difference between leverage and motivation. While motivation is an internal drive that initiates and sustains goal-directed behavior, leverage is the conscious act of using available resources, both internal and external, to evoke motivation in ourselves or others.

Why do people often procrastinate changing old habits for a long time, until suddenly they change? It's because there's a point where people "can't take it anymore" and decide to take the step forward. When the problem or pain is big enough to trigger action, internal motivation arises—in this case, "away-from" motivation. It's when the pain of sitting down to prepare for the test becomes lower compared to the greater pain of sitting in the test unprepared. The key that triggers change in humans is motivation—and the good news is, we can be proactive about it through leverage.

Leverage makes the difference between people who take important decisions and make significant changes instantly, versus those who procrastinate for years. This applies to situations in business, relationships, and all areas of life. The same applies in therapy and coaching. It's what distinguishes good from outstanding—when a person can consistently motivate themselves, and even better, help create leverage in others. That makes a great leader and a great coach.

Creating Leverage through Pleasure and Pain

The key drivers of human motivation, and what creates leverage, are pleasure and pain—or using our analogy: the carrot and the stick. Our brains constantly seek to minimize pain and maximize pleasure. Evolutionarily, the drive to avoid pain is stronger than the drive to experience pleasure. Think of it this way: when a mammoth or tiger was attacking, the motivation to survive had to be stronger than the anticipation of spending family time in the cave.

Let's look deeper into this. A client of mine was stuck in their job and kept complaining repeatedly—instead of changing jobs or shifting their perspective. The reason? First, his need structure prioritized certainty very highly. We can generate the most powerful leverage by understanding what our major needs are. Second, he had grown accustomed to his uncomfortable situation. The pain he associated with leaving this uncomfortable "comfort zone" felt much bigger than the eventual pain of realizing how much time he'd wasted being unfulfilled. He also hadn't connected with the potential pleasure of doing work he loved—his focus was elsewhere. This is a common scenario.

To zoom out and extract more learnings from this scenario: it's important to be conscious and proactive about creating leverage because, by nature, any change brings uncertainty which often feels uncomfortable. In moments of change, we enter new territories, leave our emotional homes, face new challenges, and require and build new levels of confidence—and to do that, we need both push and pull.

Why we Must Continuously Create Leverage

As we grow and expand, new challenges and opportunities arise, and we need to create leverage to tackle them. Consider a balloon with tiny holes punctured by a needle—as air enters and the balloon expands, these holes become more visible. This expanding balloon is a metaphor for us humans, and the holes represent our natural flaws and challenges that may surface as we grow. For example, this could be an uncertainty or a belief such as "I am not enough." This might not have been an issue for a long time—but in a new, larger environment, challenges or beliefs like this might come to the surface—like the expanded holes in the balloon.

The key is to recognize this as a natural part of growth and learning. We need to understand that these holes may naturally appear as we expand, but we must also work on them consciously. This relates to the importance of working with our mindset in general, and specifically to the importance of leverage. Anticipate the resistance that may arise when you face these holes, and be aware of the power of leverage to help you tackle them and lay the foundation for further growth.

Exercise:

1. *Think about a limiting belief you wrote down previously. What would be the worst possible consequences if you do not change it? Write down these consequences and feel their impact on you. This will create "away-from" leverage.*
2. *Now connect with a more beneficial belief that you developed. What would your future look like if you truly embodied this new belief and lived by the new standard every day? Write down the most positive consequences and*

deeply connect with them. This will create pull-leverage.

Fundamental 15: To maximize your motivation to act or to change, create powerful leverage by deeply connecting with both the pain of staying stuck and the pleasure of your desired future.

1.14 The Power Identity and Why "Who Am I" makes all the difference

How we define our identity, both consciously and subconsciously, is crucial for our outcomes in life. One of the strongest forces within our personality is the need to remain consistent with how we define ourselves. Indeed, there is no stronger drive than staying consistent with our self-definition, whether positive or negative. A shift in our identity can create profound changes in who we are.

Our identity is the answer to the question "Who am I?" In this sense, identity encompasses our self-image: what we perceive about ourselves becomes what we believe about ourselves. Our identity reflects the core beliefs and values we define for ourselves.

Let's use Robert Dilts' logical levels of human transformation as a reference, which illustrates the power of identity. In his pyramid, higher levels always influence the levels below. As you can see, a shift in identity can transform a person's values and beliefs, strategies and capabilities, behaviors, and ultimately the environment they choose to create. The only lever that's even more powerful is a sense of purpose, belonging, or spirituality— which influences a person's identity and all layers beneath.

Purpose and Belonging

Identity

Beliefs and Values

Capabilities and Strategies

Behavior

Environment

How can we proactively apply this concept? One simple yet powerful approach is through speaking affirmations. To gain clarity about that identity, you can connect with your future-self or "highest self," whether through a coaching session or meditation. Connect with that future self and fully immerse yourself in the experience. When you're completely in that state, answer the question: "Who am I?" Consider how people who admire your achievements would describe you. Then, bring that identity into the present and condition yourself to fully embody it.

Fundamental 16: Your identity drives your life's outcomes—consciously choose who you are, then embody that higher version of yourself daily by manifesting it and living accordingly.

1.15 The 5-Step Mindset Transformation Process

Now that you've learned the fundamentals of mindset transformation through these 14 chapters, let me share a mental framework you can use. The framework is simple, yet you can extend it with many elements you've learned so far in the SUCCESS FUNDAMENTALS book.

1. **Tell the truth.** If you've procrastinated on something important, such as a necessary job change, speak it out. If you're overweight and unfit, acknowledge it. If you're not living up to your full potential and keep distracting yourself, be honest with yourself.

2. **Make necessary changes.** To do this, you must make it a **MUST**. Define your new standards that will drive you toward achieving these goals. **Make the decision** and take full ownership. Obstacles will appear as you grow, so stay committed to your path. Link enough **pain** to not changing, whether it's a belief or an unbeneficial way to meet your needs.

3. **Break old patterns.** Interrupt the neural connections and external cues that make you hold onto old beliefs and strategies.

4. **Create new patterns.** Be proactive and try new approaches. Ideally, model successful people when creating new standards for yourself, adopting new mindset patterns, and implementing new strategies.

5. **Practice consistently.** Ensure whatever you change gets deeply embedded. Make these your fundamentals: connecting with your strengths and passions, visiting your emotional palace, listening to emotional messages, practicing your state, choosing your values, reinforcing positive beliefs, creating leverage, and connecting with your highest identity.

Creating Your Own List of FUNDAMENTALS

I encourage you to create your own list of fundamental principles for success. You can use a simple spreadsheet—or email info@bright-minds.io to get our complete list of SUCCESS FUNDAMENTALS, which you can extend with your own.

Your fundamentals can become your treasure chest of success. When truly integrated, they'll connect with your body, mind, heart, and spirit. Through these fundamentals, you ensure adherence to certain standards while nurturing yourself— which you'll explore more in later chapters. Once started, your fundamentals of success and fulfillment can continuously evolve as you learn and grow more consciously than ever before.

Next Steps with Bright Minds

Before starting the second chapter: if you're wondering how to explore your mindset more deeply and condition it for maximum success, Bright Minds offers several options. Our SUCCESS HABITS program delves deeper into specific aspects of mindset development through an 8-12 week group coaching program, with up to 6 months of accountability community support. You'll also gain access to the Bright Minds App and accountability tracking system.

Additionally, you can pursue 1:1 coaching to break through obstacles, heal, or work on your success in a highly personalized manner. Our system and coaches will hold you accountable for whatever breakthrough you want to create. Also, ask about our MindsetMaps assessment for a scientific analysis of your mindset at meta, macro, and micro levels.

PHASE 2: VISION, PURPOSE AND GOALS

In the first chapter, you learned important basics including principles from Neuro-Linguistic Programming (NLP), or practical psychology, and may have decided to consider a new or expanded model of reality. The next step is to link all of this to what truly matters to you—to ensure you're moving in the right direction.

Some of my clients come to me asking for exactly this—guidance on how to find their true mission and purpose. They may be very wealthy and able to afford most things that contribute to their high-standard life. Yet they're missing that spark, that ultimate purpose and flame that brings real fulfillment.

Then there are clients who already have clarity about where they want to go and why, but want to discover better ways to get there. Even if you're in this second group, I encourage you to go through this chapter with full focus, as you might gain even more clarity about your life mission and purpose. Remember that these are fundamentals—any opportunity to connect, apply, and reflect on them is important. It makes sense to regularly examine our life vision, mission, and purpose because they constantly evolve, and we can always make new distinctions.

Before diving into this next part, let me highlight three important points for context:

1. The feelings and motivations we experience consistently are aspects we can be proactive about, as we just learned. This includes your passions.
2. Your purpose might be related to your passion, but not necessarily. When they do align, this fusion can release tremendous life energy, as we'll explain shortly.
3. Purpose is something we may have or find—but most importantly, we can create it by actively focusing on it.

2.1 About Purpose, Goals, Mission, Vision and Values

How do all these components work together? Let me explain this based on the framework below. Your **Purpose** is your highest virtue: <u>Why</u> you exist, what you are here for, and what you ultimately strive for in life. Your **Goals** are measurable outcomes you can track to fulfill your Purpose and Vision, derived from your Mission and Vision. They define <u>What</u> you can measure yourself against to fulfill your Purpose and Vision. Your **Mission** reflects <u>What</u> you do on a daily basis to fulfill your Purpose and Vision. Your **Vision** defines your <u>What</u> and where you aspire to be in the future to fulfill your Purpose. Your **Values and Beliefs** are the standards that guide your decisions and behavior on a daily basis—they reflect <u>How</u> you achieve your Purpose.

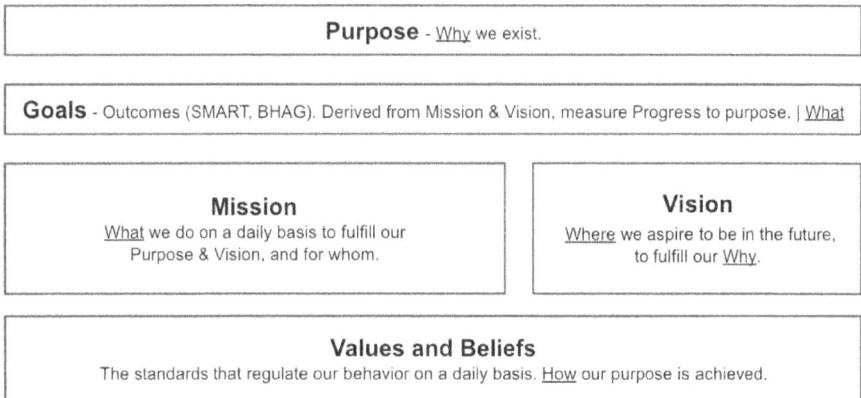

> **Purpose** - <u>Why</u> we exist.

> **Goals** - Outcomes (SMART, BHAG). Derived from Mission & Vision, measure Progress to purpose. | <u>What</u>

> **Mission**
> <u>What</u> we do on a daily basis to fulfill our Purpose & Vision, and for whom.

> **Vision**
> <u>Where</u> we aspire to be in the future, to fulfill our <u>Why</u>.

> **Values and Beliefs**
> The standards that regulate our behavior on a daily basis. <u>How</u> our purpose is achieved.

2.2 Purpose and the Big "WHY" Question

Per definition, purpose means what you stand for and why you do what you do. A person's life purpose may originate from different sources or experiences, encompass various nuances, and evolve over time. Living a purposeful life is, first and foremost, an emotional state. We can connect with that emotion by remembering purposeful moments and strengthening that feeling. To be more conscious and purposeful in each moment, we can bring up that feeling and consciously decide to give more meaning to things—to events and ultimately to our life. So we have three elements: connecting with the emotion of meaning, giving more meaning to each moment, and deciding what meaning we want to give.

What is My Purpose in Life?

To help you get closer to your WHY, let me share some best practices. When I first explored this question deeply for myself, and later when coaching clients who frequently raised the same concern, I discovered several powerful approaches. While this work can be particularly effective in coaching sessions, there are also ways to explore it independently.

The most important key is asking yourself the right questions. YOu can do that in moments of reflection, self-dialogue, and inspiration, such as when reading transformative books or inspiring seminars. The second key is reflecting with mentors and coaches. The "Why" question helps—think of a moment you love, then repeatedly ask yourself "why" or "for what." Here are six ways to explore your purpose, which will also help you define your vision (our focus in the next chapter):

1. Decide that you live a purposeful life. Create the mental space for that purpose to arise and evolve. Adopt the identity of someone who is purpose-driven. Say to yourself: "I am a purpose-driven person. I create more and more clarity about my life's purpose every day."

2. Purpose is something you create rather than find. Think of your unique life story, everything you've been through, and how you grew and evolved from these situations. Think of your passions and the moments when you enter complete emotional flow. Consider times when you've contributed to other human beings, and seek to identify patterns.

3. Regularly create space in your calendar to connect with your passions and ideal identity. Ask yourself questions like "What do I want to contribute? What do I want to build? What do I want to create? What is the ultimate state or thing that I want to create? What do I want to leave in this world?" Write down your answers.

4. As you develop a better sense of purpose, speak with mentors and people you admire. Ask them about their life purpose, and gather input and inspiration. Share your purpose with them and welcome their feedback.

5. In almost all cases, a person's purpose is about contributing to something bigger than ourselves. Whether it's helping other human beings through difficult times, creating a beautiful life for ourselves and our families, or helping and preserving our beautiful planet. Consider what contributions you want to make and how you want to grow on that journey.

6. Finally, write down your purpose, along with your vision and mission. Create a personal mission statement of one or several sentences, and a personal mission declaration that includes more nuances and details.

As highlighted in the fifth point, purpose typically relates to fulfilling our higher and spiritual needs—which are personal growth and contribution beyond ourselves. This makes sense from both a systemic and spiritual perspective. All elements in the universe are holons connected to other holons, where different parts are interconnected and ideally contributing to the good of the overall system, which in turn reflects in the prosperity of the individual parts.

Exercise:
Brainstorm and write down whatever comes to mind, when you think of your own life purpose.

Fundamental 17: Purpose is both something you feel and something you create—decide to be a purposeful person, and live a life of meaning.

2.3 Aligning Passion and Purpose: The Foundation for Lasting Success

Passion is a term we've encountered several times throughout this book, but let's examine it more deeply. The Oxford Dictionary defines passion as an intense desire or enthusiasm for something, coupled with strong emotions. As Richard Branson puts it, it's the "expression of wanting to live life to the full." Passion can serve as the foundation for both entrepreneurial and intrapreneurial mindsets, enabling intense focus and energy toward our goals.

However, passion alone isn't enough—it must align with your purpose to create sustainable inner drive and energy. Jeff Bezos emphasizes this point: "Do something you're very passionate about," but warns against trying to "chase what is kind of the hot passion of the day." While conventional wisdom suggests following your passion, it's crucial to consider how it aligns with your broader purpose and vision.

Understanding Passion Through Personal Experience

Let me share a personal example. Throughout my youth, I was passionate about football, playing 4-5 times per week. Should I have designed my life around football for the long term? This question prompts valuable reflection. Looking back, I can analyze why I developed this passion. In my small hometown, options were limited—you either joined the music club or the football club. In my worldview at the time, music was "uncool," and football satisfied many of my fundamental needs.

Football positively shaped me—developing my team spirit, nurturing my ambition, and teaching me to show up even in uncomfortable situations. However, there came a point when I realized it no longer aligned with my evolving purpose and vision. I gradually transitioned to playing occasionally with friends, and eventually stopped altogether. Would I still feel passionate playing today? Absolutely.

Analyzing the Deeper Meaning of Our Passions

There's a lot to explore about ourselves when we look at our passions more closely. Let me continue with my personal example about football. For starters, let's analyze three key points: what needs it met, my model of the world, and the emotions behind it.

1. It met all of my six needs—certainly the four personal needs on a large scale. But looking more closely, it even met the higher needs to some extent. It fulfilled my need for growth by enhancing my ability to thrive in uncertainty, take responsibility, lead a team, fail and stand up again, communicate effectively, work as part of a team, help others and receive help, and reach breakthroughs. It even met my need for contribution because I could serve the team and bring enjoyment to spectators.
2. My model of the world was simple: football was the sport that the cool kids played. Plus, there weren't many alternatives in my environment.
3. I experienced powerful emotions of excitement, achievement, and breakthrough.

When looking at this reflection—which is a way of chunking it up and examining the bigger meaning behind it—I see many points that still matter to me today. The key insight is this: when we connect with our passions and analyze them at a higher level, we often discover profound insights about what truly matters to us. We can then connect these dots with additional information to uncover insights about our purpose. Armed with this understanding of what drives our passions and how they relate to our purpose, we can then chunk down again to discover new passions that align with our core values.

Sometimes we navigate this process intuitively, naturally finding new passions that serve us and align with our purpose. However, this isn't always the case, and people often risk pursuing activities that don't truly serve them. While one could argue this exploration is simply part of life's learning journey —and I wouldn't disagree—this book provides key insights to accelerate your path forward. Our goal is to help you reach your destination faster, ensure it's truly where you want to be, and make the journey enjoyable along the way. To summarize: purpose is bigger than passion. Explore what's behind your passion, so you can focus on something that is aligned with your vision and purpose.

Fundamental 18: Passion must align with purpose to create sustainable success and fulfillment. Examine what lies behind your passions. Be open to creating new ones that truly serve your purpose and vision.

2.4 Vision: Begin with the End in Mind

Your vision is your aspirational picture of the future—where you see yourself going and what you want your life to ultimately become. It represents your desired long-term impact and legacy, painting a clear and compelling picture of what you want to create and achieve in your lifetime. Your vision represents what you want to create. It is the answer to questions such as: What do you want to create in life—for yourself, the people you love, society, and the environment?

How Reality Is Created

Everything we call reality—whether it's a product, monument, business partnership, service, or even a relationship—once started with a mental image. Consider the simple analogy of an architect: they first envision a building, then develop that image in detail, and finally create a plan to make it reality. Think about your own life. You likely have many examples where you had a dream that seemed unattainable at first. Yet, like the architect's building, you found ways to make it real.

Creating a Compelling Vision

Whatever the outcome, the first step is always to imagine it in your mind. The more clearly and vividly you imagine it with all your senses, the more real it becomes to your unconscious mind, which will help guide you there through intuition. Make your vision compelling, make it outrageous, make it worthwhile. Thinking big serves two crucial purposes. First, it generates stronger motivation and enthusiasm for putting in the work. Second, it forces your mind, including your unconscious, to devise innovative ways to achieve it. These are core ideas in Dan

Sullivan's book "10X Is Easier Than 2X." So dare to think big—because even if you don't achieve the full outcome or need more time than expected, a sufficiently ambitious vision means that even partial achievement will be deeply rewarding. We often limit ourselves by thinking too small. As Napoleon Hill states in "Think and Grow Rich": "Whatever the mind can conceive and believe, it can achieve."

Fundamental 19: Create a compelling vision by thinking big and imagining your desired outcome in vivid detail. Every reality starts with a clear mental image. Manifest that vision by revisiting it regularly.

2.5 Vision: Destination and Direction

Vision consists of two parts. One is the end goal or destination. The other is direction, which you can think of as a compass needle. Your end goals and destination don't have to be completely clear. Of course, the more vivid and colorful your destination is, the more it may compel and motivate you. And the more your mind will perceive it as reality, subconsciously following clues to make it happen, matching your internal blueprint with the outside world.

However, having a clear direction aligned with your purpose is already very powerful and will move you toward your goal. And when you think about it—the destination may change over time, but it remains important that we move in a clear and good direction every day. The distinction between vision and direction became very clear to me through my MindsetMaps coaching training and work with clients.

So what does this mean for you? If you don't have full clarity on your vision, this is fine—you can work on that along the process. But you don't have to worry, as long as you're moving in the right direction. And then, along the process, simply create mental space and possibility to develop your vision—as concrete as you want to make it. A good starting point is to create your vision board and iterate on it. Iteration means that once you've created it, connect with your vision every day—but also regularly reflect on it and ensure it (still) aligns with your life purpose.

"It's incredibly easy to work harder and harder at climbing the ladder of success, only to discover that it's leaning against the wrong wall."
— STEPHEN R. COVEY

Fundamental 20: Vision combines destination and direction—while your goals may evolve and your approaches may adapt, maintaining a clear direction aligned with purpose ensures progress.

2.6 Connecting with Your Vision Increases Your Potential and Motivation

Vision can be a powerful tool. It enhances your focus and transforms your beliefs about your capabilities and the outcomes you can create—thus expanding your potential. By visualizing your desired outcomes each morning, you can anticipate and prepare yourself for the day. You'll be intrigued by how often your mental images become reality, sometimes in even better ways than imagined. Vision becomes most powerful when you make it a multi-dimensional experience. Rather than just holding a mental image, step into that future vision with all your senses. Experience what you see, feel, and hear. Sense what you smell and taste in that moment when you've made it reality.

I remember Tony Robbins speaking about Andre Agassi, one of his coaching clients. When Andre stepped on the tennis court, it was as if he owned it. He was so certain of victory—in his focus, physiology, and language. Even thinking about stepping on the court, he was pumped with certainty to win. When Andre won Wimbledon in 1992, it matched his exact vision. As Tony described it, Andre Agassi "won Wimbledon at least 5,000 times—he had vividly visualized it since he was 5 years old." He didn't just visualize it—he immersed himself in that anticipated moment of victory in a multi-dimensional way.

But even activating just your visual capacity is powerful. Let's do a short exercise:

1. Stand straight. Close your eyes and extend your arm in front of you, pointing your finger at something you see. Now turn to the right, keeping your arm straight, as far as you can. Open your eyes and note where your

finger points. Remember that spot.

2. Return to your starting position. You can relax your arm for a moment if you'd like. Take some deep breaths. Close your eyes. Now visualize turning your body and arm again, but this time, imagine getting twice as far. Visualize reaching much further in the turn. See it, feel it with certainty.

3. Now raise your arm again and point it forward. Close your eyes and turn your body and arm again, as far as you can. Go even further—remember, you've just seen and experienced how far you can reach.

4. Open your eyes. How much further did you get? In most cases, I see people reach 30-50% further.

This is a practical demonstration of vision's power. Make sure you use it. And believe in that vision. Watch this 2:28 video interview with football player Apollos Hester, which perfectly summarizes what we've learned about the power of believing in your vision:

https://www.youtube.com/watch?v=X7ymriMhoj0

Exercise: Imagine you are your future self, living in the most compelling future you can envision.

1. *Write down what you see: What have you created for yourself? What have you created for the people around you? What impact have you made?*

2. *Create your vision board: Collect images that represent your future vision. Arrange them in a way that inspires you. Include both personal achievements and your impact on others.*

Fundamental 21: Connect with your life vision and manifest your daily victories, ideally during your morning routine. By vividly experiencing your future success in your mind, you expand your capacity to achieve it in reality.

2.7 Your Mission Statement

A mission defines what you do on a daily basis to fulfill your purpose and achieve your vision. It answers the questions of "what" you do and "for whom," providing clarity about your focus and actions. It also answers the "how" question on a higher level, which derives from your values and beliefs. Metaphorically speaking: Your purpose is like the magnetic force that directs the compass needle, and your vision is the needle and the pole it points to. Then your mission encompasses what you do to follow that magnetic force.

A person's mission is typically expressed in a mission statement. Stephen Covey calls this a "Personal Constitution." Many entrepreneurs have defined both personal and professional mission statements. You can do this whether you're an entrepreneur or an intrapreneur.

- The personal mission is an overarching statement, with Purpose as the foundation and focusing on Vision, including nuances of what you do and how you achieve it.
- The professional mission includes Purpose and Vision, as well as what you do and how you achieve it, in slightly more detail.

These are suggestions—there are many ways to formulate your mission statement. You can decide whether you need one or two, and how high-level or detailed they should be. Every individual and organization has their own preferences. What's important is that your mission sounds compelling and clear: like a North Star that provides guidance for your daily decisions, actions, and focus. A mission statement should highlight your Purpose and Vision, compelling enough to motivate action.

To give you an example, here are my mission statement and that of Bright Minds:

- **Personal Mission Statement from Tilman Resch:** Inspire, educate and empower people to live a long and truly fulfilled life which they desire, and to become their best selves. Simultaneously, bring growth, prosperity and wealth to the loving family I will co-create, enough for generations to come.
- **Company Mission Statement of Bright Minds:** To help over 10 million people and thousands of organizations maximize their outcomes, while creating a path of meaning, growth, contribution and fulfillment.

Exercise:
Write down the first version of your own mission statement.

Fundamental 22: Create a compelling mission statement that captures your purpose and vision—let it serve as your daily guide for decisions and actions that move you toward your highest aspirations.

2.8 Goal Setting is a Continuous Process

Your goals are specific, measurable outcomes to achieve within a certain timeframe. They are derived from your mission and vision statements and serve as benchmarks for measuring progress toward fulfilling your purpose. Setting goals is important and helpful because the process itself is a way of manifesting your outcomes and directing your focus. The process makes sense even if you're not totally clear about your purpose, vision and mission (in fact, most people have much more clarity about this than they think they have).

Having clear goals will increase your persistence and self-efficacy, making you less susceptible to the undermining effects of anxiety, disappointment, and frustration. It also makes it easier to evaluate your progress toward where you want to go and make adjustments along the way. This applies to any personal and professional area of your life.

Your goals must be well defined. You may know the notion of SMART goals: Specific, Measurable, Actionable, Realistic (yet stretching), and Time-based. In addition, follow the principle of BHAG—make your goals Big, Hairy, and Audacious Goals, which means they should be bold and compelling. Well-defined goals prompt our mind and help us create strategies to achieve them, using our conscious and subconscious mind.

Connect with your goals regularly, as goal setting is a fundamental in itself. Remain flexible about adjusting your goals, and make it a continuous process that you do at least annually, and ideally quarterly.

Exercise: Take some time for yourself, ideally in morning hours and/

or after a workout session when your body is activated. Even better, meditate before you start.

1. *Write down any goals that come to your mind for 15 minutes. Include personal, professional, and material goals.*
2. *Label these goals according to timeline: 1/3/5/20 years.*
3. *Pick the top three goals for each category and write down one action you commit to doing in the next 12 hours toward each goal.*

Outlook to Planning and Execution

Goals significantly increase the likelihood of success because our conscious and unconscious minds are programmed to move toward something. However, this is only truly effective when you also create a plan to act upon it and take first actions immediately—show your mind that you really mean it.

Fundamental 23: Set clear goals following the SMART and BHAG principles. Connect with them regularly, ensure both planning and action are part of the process—while maintaining flexibility to adapt goals and execution approaches.

2.9 Calibrating your Compass

If you want to dive even deeper into creating your purpose, declaration, vision board, and mission statement, you can work with a Bright Minds coach or join the SUCCESS HABITS program. Creating clarity about these aspects is one of our strengths and core ways we help our clients.

PHASE 3: PRIORITIZATION, ACTION AND HABITS

You've done the inner work - transforming your mindset and gaining clarity on your purpose, vision, and goals. Now comes the crucial step: taking action. While mindset shapes our potential, only consistent action turns that potential into extraordinary success and fulfillment.

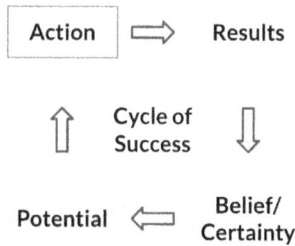

```
  ┌─────────┐
  │ Action  │  ⇨     Results
  └─────────┘

          Cycle of
    ⇑     Success     ⇓

  Potential  ⇦     Belief/
                   Certainty
```

Remember the circle of success from Chapter 1? Action is one of the driving forces. And while we'll explore this deeper later in the book, consider how trial, error, and correction accelerate this cycle, enhancing every component of success.

3.1 The Four Dimensions of Time: Transform Busy into Purposeful

Why is prioritization important? Time is our most valuable asset, yet most people don't value it accordingly. Many even complain about not having enough time - while, upon conscious reflection, they'd realize how much time they waste on activities that don't align with what truly matters in their lives. A recent study showed that the average Netflix user spends 3.2 hours per day streaming, while the average American spends almost 2.5 hours on social media daily. In this section, you will learn how to categorize and prioritize your activities to spend your time more consciously—whether that's working on your purpose and mission, spending time with loved ones, or pursuing whatever brings you true fulfillment through growth and contribution.

The Eisenhower Matrix, popularized by Stephen Covey as the Time Matrix, provides a powerful framework for conscious time allocation. It divides our activities into four distinct quadrants:

1. *The Zone: These are important activities that are not urgent. They include working on high-impact goals, proactive work, creative thinking, planning and prevention, relationship building, learning, and renewal and recreation. These activities help us truly grow and expand.*
2. *Dimension of Demand: These are important activities that are urgent. They include pressing problems, unforeseen events, emergency meetings, and crises. Although the pressure may sometimes be helpful to "get things done," spending too much time here can drain our energy.*
3. *Dimension of Delusion: These are unimportant activities that are urgent. They include unnecessary reports,*

needless interruptions, irrelevant meetings, other people's minor issues, unimportant emails and tasks, phone calls, and status posts. Due to time and social pressure, people often feel obligated to comply and sense contribution, although most of these activities are truly a waste of time.

4. **Dimension of Distraction**: These are unimportant activities that are non-urgent. They include trivial work, avoidance activities, excessive relaxation, social media, Netflix, television, gaming, internet browsing, time-wasters, and gossip. Any time spent here is truly wasted.

Eisenhower Matrix for Prioritization

Exercise: Reflect on Your Weekly Time Allocation. Track and analyze the activities from your past 7 days:

1. Create a list of all your activities in Excel or Google Docs.
2. For each activity, add:
   o Time spent (in hours)

- Quadrant category (Q1-Q4)
3. *Reflect and Plan:*
    - *Identify activities to reduce or eliminate. Calculate the hours you could reclaim.*
    - *Choose which high-value activities deserve this reclaimed time*

FUNDAMENTAL 24: Time is your most precious asset. Prioritize ruthlessly by spending most of your time on important, non-urgent activities that drive real growth and fulfillment.

3.2 Enhancing Consciousness About the Value of Time

Prioritizing the right actions in your limited time is crucial not only for your outcomes and success but also for your sense of fulfillment. If you spend lots of time in the Delusion and Distraction zones, both your conscious and subconscious mind will likely send you signals that something is off. These might be more obvious, especially your conscious mind causing thought cycles about spending your time differently. And they can be more subtle and less concrete - that's when you know something isn't right, your subconscious knows, and expresses it through a bad conscience.

To stay on track, the best practice is simple: assess your time management regularly as part of your weekly reflection—until you embody the concept so thoroughly that it becomes an unconscious competence, like driving a car.

Advanced time management and prioritization habits not only serve you, but you can be an example for others. You'll inspire others when they see how great you must be in "the zone". And soon they'll ask you about it, or you can proactively share what works well for you - or even start a culture initiative around that topic. For example, at home, establish a joint reading time with your partner. Or in your business, create focus time slots for your team to concentrate on highly important activities.

Taking control of your time will soon reflect in outcomes larger than you can imagine. When appreciating your time with meaningful activities becomes your new standard, you're showing appreciation to the god/universe/life or whatever you believe in - and you will get rewarded. You'll likely be more conscious in anything you do, remember how you do one thing is how you do everything. And you'll attract more successful people who also truly appreciate time.

The Difference Between Renewal and Distraction

Are watching Netflix or using social media always "bad" activities? It's important to look at this with nuance rather than seeing it as black and white. Watching a movie consciously, appreciating it as a piece of art, for a limited time, can be a highly nurturing and self-renewing activity. Similarly, texting someone on social media can be a way to connect, communicate, and nurture a relationship. However, be very deliberate about these nuances, because in reality, the way most people use these mediums is actually distracting rather than renewing.

Fundamental 25: Your mind knows when you're wasting time - listen to both conscious thoughts and subtle feelings of unease as signals to realign with meaningful activities.

3.3 The Architecture of Habits: Building Your Success Routines

Many of the activities you reflected on are probably things you do on a regular basis: we call those <u>habits</u>. A habit is an automatic reaction to a specific situation. It's something that we've done so repeatedly that it has gone on autopilot. While you're probably very familiar with what habits are, in this book we'll focus on three practical aspects: the reasons why we adopt habits, the structure of habits, and how to change them. And of course, we'll include an exercise.

To illustrate the importance of habits, let's contrast two ways to start a day:

1. Bad habits: Snoozing the alarm three times before finally getting up, grabbing your phone first thing in the morning and scrolling through social media for 10 minutes, eating a croissant, and rushing to work.
2. Good habits: Getting up early after a good night of sleep, making your bed, drinking two glasses of water, doing a short exercise, meditating, reading, visualizing and writing; then using your state of clarity and focus for an "in the zone" activity.

Types of Habits

There are different reasons why we adopt habits. In more profound terms, we can relate this to Robert Dilts' logical levels —a concept in Neuro-Linguistic Programming (NLP). Based on that model, habits (Level 3) are influenced by our values/beliefs (Level 4), which are influenced by our identity (Level 5), which in turn is influenced by our purpose or belonging. Habits, on the other hand, determine our actions/behaviors (Level 2), which determine the environment we create (Level 1).

For practicality, we'll work with James Clear's definition from his bestselling book "Atomic Habits." Clear distinguishes three types of habits:

1. **Identity-driven habits:** These are behaviors we perform because they align with who we believe we are. The driving force is that we tend to stay consistent with our identity.
2. **Process-driven habits:** These stem from the conviction that establishing a new routine or standard consistently will move us in a beneficial direction. We can also call these standard-driven habits.
3. **Goal-driven habits:** These relate to specific goals for a defined period. If the habit is beneficial, it's recommended to convert it into a process-driven or identity-driven habit, either during the process or after achieving the goal.

How Habits are Structured

At this point, let's create a deeper understanding of what habits consist of—which will enable you to change and adjust them more intuitively. Habits consist of four elements: cue, craving, response, and reward.

- The **cue** is what triggers the brain to notice an opportunity for a reward. A cue can be a smell, a sound, an event, an interaction, or anything else that triggers a desire.
- The **craving** is the emotional relevance attached to a certain cue. When you notice the cue, the brain anticipates an opportunity for a change in your physical or emotional state. You crave the satisfaction that the change will bring, and this craving is what prompts you to take action.

- The **response** is the behavior or habit you perform to elicit the change you desire. Your brain prompts you to take a certain action it believes will create the feeling of satisfaction you want.
- The **reward** is the satisfaction you gain from the action you take. You have successfully satisfied your craving and changed your physical or emotional state. The brain then builds a pathway from the cue to this state of pleasure. Every time you experience the same cue, the brain will be triggered to desire that pleasure again. You'll be prompted to perform the same action, thereby creating a habit.

Fundamental 26: Your habits are a reflection of who you are, and they determine your outcomes in life. Understand where existing habits come from, and what causes them. Regularly choose to transform your set of habits.

3.4 How to Change Habits

You can use the four elements of habits proactively to create new ones and break undesired ones. Before making any changes, remember the lessons from previous chapters. When replacing a habit, ensure that:

- Your needs will be met through the new behavior in a stronger, more sustainable way
- The new habit aligns with your purpose and outcomes
- You create the necessary leverage

We can call this creating the right context for habit transformation.

With the right context in place, focus on the transformation itself. Consider all four factors when changing habits. Here's how to create a new habit (to eliminate negative habits, reverse these steps, e.g. make it unnoticeable):

1. Make the **cue** noticeable: Put the sports bag next to your door, or stack your new activity on top of another activity you're already doing.
2. Make the **craving** appealing: Anchor a positive emotion to the activity.
3. Make the **response** easy/simple: While building the habit, start with a shorter version of it.
4. Make the **reward** fulfilling/satisfying: Include emotional rewards during and after the process..

Exercise:

1. *Think of one positive habit you would like to adopt.*
2. *Define why it is important to you and what the consistent behavior will bring.*
3. *Design your new habit using these four elements.*

Fundamental 27: Transform your habits by working with their building blocks (cue, craving, response and reward). Make cues noticeable or invisible, cravings appealing or unattractive, responses easy or difficult, and rewards satisfying or unfulfilling.

3.5 Secret to Lasting Habitual Change

There are two additional important fundamentals for lasting change we'll cover here. The first relates to the power of belonging and identity, and the second to the power of embodying that identity.

Imagine a football fan, John, who truly identifies with Chelsea London. He would feel a sense of belonging and say "I am a fan." He would adopt beliefs and values that other football fans share, learn players' names and club songs, sing in the stadium, and habitually read articles about the team. He would regularly attend matches or visit fan clubs—without anyone needing to tell him.

Or imagine Anna working at Amazon Web Services, which has a strong company culture. She would consider herself an "Amazonian." She would adopt and live by the company's values, the 16 Leadership Principles. She would show up and act like a leader, investing extra hours to help customers. She would habitually research technology topics—without anyone having to tell her.

The most powerful drivers in habitual change are senses of higher purpose, belonging, and identity. Adjusting or reconnecting with your identity is the most practical lever you can use. Note that when you apply it, resistance might emerge from one level above, related to your purpose or belonging. For example, someone wanting to be a non-smoker might fear losing their belonging to other smokers and thereby losing a way to fulfill their need for love and connection. Remember that different forces play a role when resistance emerges.

Fully Embody Your New Identity for Lasting Change

To install or strengthen a positive identity that facilitates positive habits, you can apply manifesting through visualization and/or affirmations. When doing this, be mindful of what was mentioned earlier: if you truly want to embody and maximize the transformation, engage all your senses, as highlighted in the chapter about the TRIAD. When you involve all senses—seeing it, saying it, feeling it, even smelling and tasting it—you create what Tony Robbins calls "incantations," that multidimensional way to engage your entire being. Ultimately, positive energy prevails and outlives any negative energy if we nurture it enough. Through this newly defined identity, you manifest your habitual shift and make it lasting.

Fundamental 28: The biggest behavioral change results from shifts in identity. Embody your new identity fully by experiencing it with all senses when you manifest it. Your habits will naturally align with who you choose to become.

3.6 Managing Fundamental Routines

Now that you understand how to break and create habits, let's focus on which ones to develop. Fundamental routines consist of your morning and evening routines, along with the habits and principles you follow throughout your day. Tim Ferriss's research in "Tools of Titans" reveals a striking pattern: the vast majority of the 200 successful people he interviewed maintain consistent evening, morning, and daily routines. Let's examine the essential elements of designing these routines.

Remember our earlier example of poor habits: snoozing the alarm three times, scrolling through social media for 10 minutes, grabbing a croissant, rushing to work, and spending the first hour of the workday sorting through emails. Consider the cascading impact of these choices—how they affect your emotions, push you into a reactive rather than proactive state, and what that croissant does to your body. The quick pastry triggers an insulin spike, leading to increased food cravings and mood fluctuations, while offering no real nutritional value. This is precisely the pattern we want to break. Now, let's explore routines that will serve your success.

3.7 Your Evening Routine Determines Your Next Day's Outcomes

The way you spend your last hours before sleeping determines the quality and outcomes of your next day. Looking at ourselves as multi-dimensional beings with our body, mind, heart, and spirit—at minimum, take care of your body and mind in your evening routine. By doing so, you'll also naturally nurture your heart and spirit to some extent.

The Body: If you avoid eating in the hours before sleeping, go to bed at a consistent time, and give your body the chance to calm down and prepare for sleep (including hormone production, where blue light has a critical effect), you'll sleep better—and consequently have higher energy and mental clarity the next day.

The Mind: If you stop working at least one hour before sleeping, get some fresh air or take a walk, avoid stressful conversations, get some physical touch, reflect and write, read and study, write down what you're grateful for and what you anticipate as wins for the next day—your mind will renew overnight, process learnings better, and prepare for tomorrow's victories.

You can also go beyond these basics by including practices for your heart—like positive affirmations or physical contact with a loved one—and spirit, such as meditation, prayer, or connecting with your vision and goals for the next day.

Fundamental 29: The quality of your evening routine determines the quality of your next day. Avoid food in the 3 hours before sleeping, calm your mind in the hour before—and manifest your vision in the minutes before sleeping.

3.8 Your Morning Routine: Winning Your Day Before It Begins

See your morning routine as a way to start each day with a personal victory. It's dedicated time to renew yourself in all four dimensions of your being (body, mind, heart, and spirit). It's also time to practice important fundamentals while connecting with your life's mission and creating what you want to become.

Here are components you can include in your morning routine:

1. Get up early (whether at 4 or 6 AM is up to you, but choose a time and stay consistent). Get up with the first alarm. The statement "I'm not a morning person" is usually an excuse that requires a simple change in your habitual biorhythm.
2. Drink one to two glasses of warm water immediately after waking to hydrate your body.
3. Make your bed to create order. Remember, how you do one thing is how you do anything.
4. Practice meditation, gratitude, and visualization.
5. Complete at least a small physical exercise.
6. Write down your intention for the day.
7. Use incantations to empower your identity and best self: condition your mind for success.

Pro tip: Dedicate time for creation during or right after your morning routine. Take 2-3 hours for creation and studying/learning before 9 AM. Use this time for "in the zone" activities, such as creating strategy, writing articles, reading books, and generally activities aligned with your most important goals.

When I share my personal morning routine, people often respond in one of two ways. Some share their own routines, which inspires me. Others say "this was great but not possible for them." While I understand that life circumstances vary greatly, whenever you catch yourself saying "This is not possible" about something this beneficial, look deeper and think twice. Ask yourself the more helpful question: "How could I make it possible?"

Fundamental 30: Rise early to condition your body, mind, heart, and spirit—and begin each day with clear intention and focused creation. Include at least gratitude, manifestation, affirmations, physical activation, and writing in your ritual.

3.8 Daily Routines: Creating Standards for Excellence

Life gives us endless choices each day—the decisions we make determine the outcomes we get. Define a set of standards for yourself that serve as fundamental guardrails for how you spend your day. The goal is to keep your body energetic and nourished throughout the day and your mind clear and focused. We'll cover basics about energy management, nutrition, and maintaining mental focus in the next chapter.

Exercise

1. *Design your ideal evening and morning routines.*
2. *Life doesn't always go as planned. Create your minimum/ must routine for when you travel or when you only have 10-15 minutes.*
3. *Create a sheet or table where you will capture your daily routines and principles. You may already have some ideas about it - and write down the key points for you from the next chapter.*

Fundamental 31: Your daily routines reflect your personal standards—and together they shape the quality of your life. Make it a habit to focus on the important things, and practice self-renewal regularly.

PHASE 4: ENERGY AND FOCUS FOR EXTRAORDINARY OUTCOMES

Throughout your personal development journey in this book, we've covered mindset transformation; purpose, mission, and goals; as well as execution with action, habits, and routines. In the fourth phase of SUCCESS FUNDAMENTALS, our goal is to maximize the impact we create through our actions and the enjoyment in the process. As my mentor Blair Singer says, "You can achieve three times as much in half the time."

You will learn:

1. About the four human dimensions and how to nurture them
2. An outcome-based organization system and why it's better than just managing your to-dos
3. Ways to consistently achieve states of flow and deep work
4. Why our environment is crucial and how to create and leverage a team to maximize your impact and enjoyment
5. Concrete ways to care for your health and body—your energy and physical health are preconditions for almost everything else

Creating both impact and sustainable success requires a holistic approach. As Robert Dilts observes in Success Factor Modelling (Part 3), based on his analysis of Elon Musk's mindset: "Creating sustainable success is a matter of consciousness and balance with respect to every part of the system." Dilts refers not only to our internal human system but also to the larger entities we're part of—our communities, families, and the natural environment. As conscious leaders of our lives, we must consider both the microcosm and macrocosm, and ensure we live in harmony with them. With this context in mind, let's examine the multiple dimensions of the unique system that each of us represents.

Note: Throughout this chapter, the word "system" will be used in two distinct contexts—first, in reference to systems theory, cybernetics, and holon theory; and second, in the context of organizational systems.

4.1 The Four Human Intelligences

We humans are four-dimensional beings, consisting of body, mind, heart, and spirit, as Stephen Covey outlines in his book "The 7 Habits of Highly Effective People." Each of these dimensions holds its own intelligence:

1. **Body:** Body-based intelligence. Discipline and self-control. The ability to see things as they really are and execute.
2. **Mind:** Mental intelligence. Vision and focus. The ability to consider many solutions, synthesize, and create clear images of the targeted solution.
3. **Heart:** Emotional intelligence. Passion and dedication. This is what drives us to maintain focus and control, in service of a larger goal.
4. **Spirit:** Spiritual intelligence. Conscience and integrity. This refers to ethical principles and our ability to differentiate right from wrong in complex situations.

When we think of maximizing our output, we need two things: First, enhancing these four human intelligences. Second, maximizing energy in all four dimensions. Practicing nurturing and self-renewal of these four dimensions not only makes you more balanced, fulfilled, healthier, and energetic—it also makes you a more intelligent human being overall. Let's look at the energy aspect in more detail.

Fundamental 32: Your full potential lies in combining and integrating your four human intelligences: your body executes, your mind envisions, your heart drives, and your spirit guides.

4.2 Maximizing Energy through all 4 Human Dimensions

Let's first look at the opposite: what if we do not nurture and re-energize ourselves as human beings? As Stephen Covey puts it, "to live without self-renewal is like trying to cut a piece of wood with a dull saw." It somehow works, but it is ineffective and can even be harmful. To create consistent results, we need to habitually renew and nurture ourselves, "sharpening the saw." How to do this? You probably have ideas about it already, as these things are intuitive—nonetheless, we need to be conscious about them and prioritize spending time there:

1. **Body:** Exercising, eating healthy, breathing consciously, taking ice baths, sleeping well and sufficiently
2. **Mind:** Learning, writing, reading, and journaling
3. **Heart:** Caring relationships, quality conversations, taking time for people, caring for and loving yourself
4. **Spirit:** Inspiration, meditation, spending time in nature, thinking deeply about our mission and values, giving meaningful service

Practicing nurturing and self-renewal habitually will enhance everything else in your life positively, including your everyday decisions and relationships. It will greatly improve the quality of every hour of your day, including the depth and restfulness of your sleep. It will build long-term physical, mental, and spiritual strength that we all need to handle life's challenges.

Why Activity Aligned with Your Purpose, Mission, and Passion Creates Energy

In an earlier chapter, we discussed the importance of aligning your actions with your mission and purpose, ideally alongside your passion. This is one fundamental way to maximize your energy. As becomes clear when you look at these dimensions, purposefulness and passion align with all four dimensions, but especially with our heart and spirit. Taking purposeful and passionate action is actually a nurturing and renewal activity in itself.

Four-Dimensional Activities

Activities that contribute to all four dimensions and give you energy we call 4D-activities. Examples include: your morning routine, a conscious workout, giving someone a hug, taking deep breaths mindfully, singing a song, or consciously enjoying a healthy meal. Note the correlation with activities that fulfill all six human needs—of course depending on your map of the world.

Fundamental 33: Renew and energize all four human dimensions daily—your body, mind, heart, and spirit are the foundation of sustained excellence.

4.3 Mental Clarity versus Mental Overload

For the past 10 years, I have had side businesses alongside my studies and corporate career. There have been times when my mind was overloaded with information, tasks, and obligations. This led me through several rounds of searching for ways to organize myself well and get my mind clear. After many cycles of learning, I found what I will present to you in this book. But let's take a step back first.

Think of a moment in your life when you knew exactly what to do in the moment and what to do next—your mind was absolutely clear. You knew what you were after, with nothing else to worry about. Perhaps your mind was in an inspiring flow state, creatively thinking about how you could make your customers even happier, increase your sales, surprise a loved one, or make the win-win outcome even bigger. It feels amazing, doesn't it? This is the state of clarity we want more of.

Now think of a second moment that was quite the opposite: one of those days when your to-do list seems to stack up, everybody wants something from you, there's too much to do, and you don't know where to start. One crisis piles on top of another, and as if it wasn't bad enough that you can barely respond to all those needs, in a quiet moment you realize that most or all of the things you're doing are for someone else. In that fight-or-flight mode, the friction loss might exceed the learning. Many people nowadays often find themselves in this second scenario. They struggle with the sheer amount of responsibilities, information, to-dos, and opportunities—and have neither the time nor mental capacity to focus on what's important to them.

Fundamental 34: Mental clarity is a state of mind and an emotion. Practice your state of clarity by connecting with that feeling—and being fully present and immersed in each activity you choose to focus on.

4.4 Mind Like Water: Maximizing Clarity and Focus

We can do powerful things with our mindset, as you learned in this book—there is a whole chapter on how we can manage our state, create an identity that serves us, and create a compelling vision. But this may only take you so far if you don't have a system that keeps your mind clear and creates space for your priorities. So beyond mindset, there's another important area we shouldn't underestimate or deny: how we plan and organize our lives.

The opposite of a clear mind is a state of consciousness overloaded with information. Think of a computer analogy: A computer has two types of storage—short-term storage called RAM and "cold storage" or file system. RAM provides necessary information almost in real-time to fulfill any task. Problems occur when there's too much information in RAM—when it gets overloaded, the computer starts freezing. That's why there's also "cold storage" to store large amounts of information. It's called a file system or "cold storage" because that information is accessed less frequently and may take a few seconds to query—although nowadays this happens quite fast.

How Brain Overload Kills Dreams

Our minds work very similarly to a computer. However, most people misuse their minds, especially when it comes to using our RAM or short-term storage. People overload their brains with so many to-dos and pieces of information that they start to freeze. Then they begin to distract themselves and procrastinate, feeling stressed and saying to themselves "I'm out of here." This is when they might give up on their dreams completely.

Creating a Mind Like Water

We humans need to externalize how we manage our actions and capture snippets of information to function ideally. We need to create that "mind like water" where we can be in flow, knowing everything is in place and organized. When that's a given, we not only feel "in control," but our intuition can also perform at its peak and give us the right information when we need it. The externalization I refer to is different from creating a to-do list. Curious? The next chapter is very powerful.

Fundamental 35: Keep your mind like water: focused on what matters most, and clear from distracting thoughts. Create systems and processes to keep your mind free and focused.

4.5 Three Core Principles for Organization and Planning

The model we teach in Bright Minds draws from Tony Robbins' Outcome-Based Organization System, with which he built $9 billion in businesses and helped tens of millions of people worldwide. We also incorporate related principles. There are three fundamental principles to organize yourself—three essential elements you need whenever you want to achieve something:

1. See things as they are, not worse. Approach things with a positive mindset.
2. See things even better than they are. Create an exciting, stretch vision.
3. Create a plan to get there.

Through planning, you'll inevitably ask yourself many questions. Generally, thinking is the process of asking and answering questions. When you organize and plan, you're consciously and subconsciously evaluating and deciding—constantly asking and answering questions.

Fundamental 36: Follow the three core principles for organization and planning: First, see reality exactly as it is. Second, envision it better than it is. Third, create a clear plan to get there.

4.6 The Power of Questions

The questions we ask ourselves can make all the difference because they determine what we focus on. The first problem is that most people ask themselves poor questions all day long. The second problem is that they're not even aware of it.

People typically develop a primary question that directs their life's focus. Here are examples that highlight the contrast and importance:

1. **Unhelpful Question:** "What's wrong with me?" Note that what's wrong is always available if we focus on it. Some people feel permanently worthless, see few choices, think there are no alternatives, and believe they'll always be in pain—because that's where their focus remains.
2. **Helpful Questions:** "How can I make it better?" This leads to other questions like:
   - How can I utilize this to make the world better?
   - How do I improve myself?
   - How can I use this to become a better leader?
   - How can I help more?

Questions are the controlling force of your thinking. What you think determines what you focus on. Your focus determines how you feel—your state in the moment, which is your potential. Think of what you can be proud of. Think of what you're grateful for. Think of what you learned from any situation. Who do you love? Who loves you? This state determines the quality of your action, or whether you take action at all. It all starts with the questions you ask yourself. You'll act very differently when feeling depressed than when feeling euphoric, centered, strong, courageous, or passionate. So you must take control, and one of the most powerful ways is to ask better questions.

Exercise:

1. **What is a question you tend to focus on that doesn't serve you?** *This could be based on fears that hold you back but occupy your thoughts. The key is to formulate a better question. Spend minimal time on the problem and over 90% on the solution or outcome you want—focus on the turn you want to make.*
2. **What would be a more empowering question that could become your primary question in life?**

Fundamental 37: Ask empowering questions, because they are the foundations for the outcomes you'll achieve. Cause and effect: Your questions shape your focus, your focus determines your state, and your state drives your actions, which determine what results you get.

4.7 Relate Questions to your Outcomes

Throughout this book, we've highlighted the importance of focusing on outcomes. Let me emphasize it once more by bringing different elements together. Key to success is directing your focus to your outcome and its underlying purpose—then developing an action plan that energizes you because you're so intrigued by the outcome and purpose.

How to focus on outcomes consistently? By consistently asking questions that relate to your outcome, thereby prompting your brain strategically. This unveils an interesting parallel with GenAI: just as with this decades-old theory, the quality of prompts—the questions you ask an AI—determines the quality of outcomes.

Let's look at Bill Gates and how he translated his vision into a primary question. From Microsoft's early days, his primary question was: "How do we become the intelligence that runs all computers?" His underlying idea was that if they became the intelligence running all computers, everyone would use their products. Years later, as technology and markets changed, he adopted a new primary question: "How do we become the intelligence that runs the information superhighway?" These questions kept Microsoft employees up at night—in a good way —trying to fulfill that mission by finding and implementing answers.

Microsoft employees could then develop action plans based on a clear vision and mission. As the vision was bold and ambitious, it required new approaches—which naturally don't always work. But with a clear primary question, employees maintained their drive and found alternative paths. (Corporate culture plays a role here too, though we won't explore that.)

Selecting the Right Actions Based on Your Outcome through Questions

The right questions supercharge your effectiveness. Don't ask yourself "What do I have to do?" Rather, reflect on:

1. What is my outcome?
2. What is my purpose?
3. What actions can take me there?

Then choose the right actions. There are millions of ways to achieve something, and there's almost always an easier, more sustainable, or more effective way—if you're open to finding it. Once you've selected your actions, consider which ones are truly necessary. You've probably realized that 20% of actions bring 80% of outcomes.

When choosing actions, select those through which you'll enjoy the process. When you don't enjoy the process and feel fulfilled alongside your success—that isn't really success. As Tony Robbins says, success without fulfillment is essentially failure. After all, the difference between play and work, enjoyment and exhaustion is emotion. So it's in your hands: you can change what you do and how you feel about it.

Fundamental 38: When planning for outcomes, always start with your outcome in mind. Then ask: What is my purpose? What actions will take me there? Which path brings both success and fulfillment?

4.8 Use Questions to Trigger Innovation in Yourself and Others

All human progress is preceded by new questions and leaders often ask new questions, leading people to new answers. Think about Martin Luther King, John F. Kennedy, or Elon Musk. These are visionaries who imagined outcomes no one else had conceived and found compelling reasons to pursue them. Whether it was understanding that we are all equal, putting the first human on the moon, or truly electrifying the automobile industry—they saw possibilities others hadn't and inspired action.

Robert Kennedy had a famous borrowed quote: "Some people see things that were and ask why. I look at things that never were and ask 'Why not?'" Change your life by changing your questions. It will transform where you're going. The way you change your life is to change your thinking - at the end it's psychology.

Get unreasonable. It was unreasonable for Jeff Bezos to imagine building an everything store. But unreasonable people change the world, and you have to decide what kind of person you want to be. Successful people are often unreasonable in their expectations for themselves and what they're willing to do to succeed. Be willing to do anything to make it happen—as long as it's for the greater good.

Fundamental 39: Transform your reality by asking new questions—great leaders see possibilities where others see limits. Dare to be unreasonable in pursuit of what's possible and ask "Why not?" instead of "Why?"

4.9 Why Outcome-based Life Management

The Conventional Way to Manage Life

According to research by Timewatch in 2022, 88% of Americans use some form of to-do list system to manage their life: 38% use a dedicated to-do list, 23% schedule tasks in their calendar, 14% prioritize what's most important, and 13% use their email inbox as a task list. However, about half of the tasks never get completed. When you ask people how they feel about their to-do list and calendar, most respond that they are stressed about it.

The Outcome-Based Way to Manage Life and Why We Need It

We've emphasized the importance of focusing on outcomes. So at this point, you should realize there's a mismatch here. Is managing life by to-do lists really the appropriate way to direct one's focus? It would be clearly more helpful to focus on outcomes, instead of to-dos.

A system is needed that integrates all the elements you've learned throughout this book—one that makes you reflect about your mindset constantly, reflect about your actions, and connect with your mission consistently for all areas of life that matter to you. Why master this? To have a mechanism that moves you consistently towards the life you want—and makes you live each moment more purposefully.

My Personal History with Different Types of To-Do Lists

Personally, I had used various to-do lists, then optimized my system through the teachings of Stephen Covey and David Allen. But despite the benefits, I kept feeling stressed as tasks stacked up and got pushed to the next week, again and again.

I wasn't managing my life—I was managing my to-dos. Plus, I was regularly struggling with how I could consistently stay connected with my mission in what I do. It wasn't until I discovered the principles of purpose and outcome-based management by Tony Robbins that things really started to click. In the following chapters, you'll learn the basics of outcome-based organization.

Fundamental 40: Transform your productivity and results by managing outcomes aligned with your life's vision and purpose —instead of just managing time and tasks.

4.10 Outcome- and Purpose based Organization System (OPS)

We start by introducing the components of outcome and purpose-based life management (for simplicity, we call it OPS):

- **Life Areas of Growth:** Categories of our life to be managed. These typically include personal and professional areas and their most important outcomes. For each one, you define your purpose, vision, mission, specific role, and quarterly as well as 1-year goals.
- **Roles:** The hats you wear in each category. For example, if one of your professional areas is "purpose-driven people leader," your roles might include coach, networker, and boss. Roles can even sound unconventional, like being a "source of clarity."
- **Actions:** We could call them to-dos, but in this system we call them actions—aligning with our outcome-based philosophy. You don't have to complete all actions to reach your outcomes. However, be clear about your <u>musts</u>.
- **Action Blocks:** The simplest and clearest way to tackle any result you want to achieve. In the spirit of "beginning with the end in mind" (Stephen Covey) or "working backwards" (Jeff Bezos), you start with the result and attach a clear purpose. You then identify necessary actions, prioritize them, and put them in order.
- **Project:** If the result is more complex and requires several action blocks, you can combine them into a project. Typically, these action blocks share the same purpose and/or result.

Each action has a distinct life area of growth attached with deeper purpose and meaning. This makes each moment and action more meaningful as part of your life plan. For example, going to the gym and eating healthy become purposeful actions —to live a longer, more vital life with joyful and conscious emotions.

4.11 Defining your Areas of Focus and Growth

The initial element is defining your growth areas. We introduce here the "Wheel of Life" as a starting point to understand this way of thinking and define your categories. When reflecting on your Wheel of Life, note that each category matters. Think of a car tire: if it's not perfectly round, it won't roll well. It may move forward, but it will require much more effort. Life is similar—to reach ultimate fulfillment, we want to grow proportionally in all categories.

However, the Wheel of Life is just an exercise to help you understand this way of thinking. Based on this understanding, you can define the specific categories for your system. Personally, I have 16 categories in my system. These cover every aspect of the Wheel of Life in some way. If you're interested in my specific categories, contact me directly.

Personal Wheel of Life

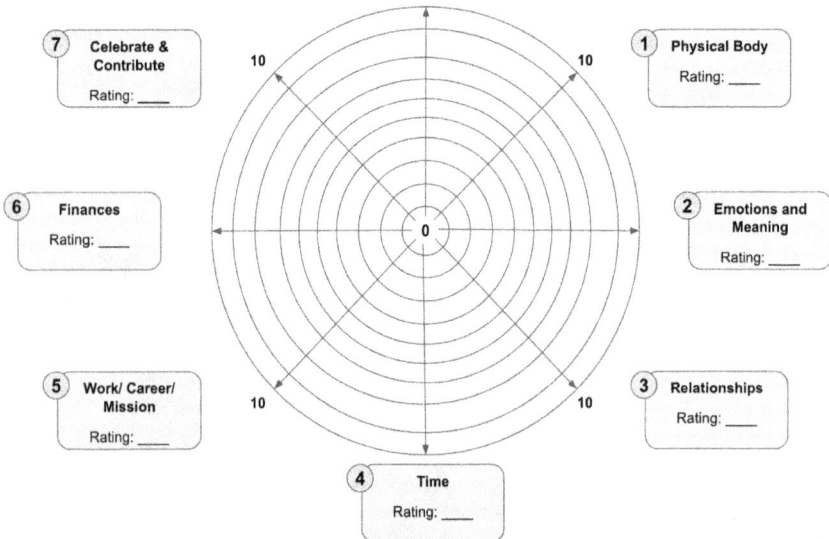

Professional Wheel of Life

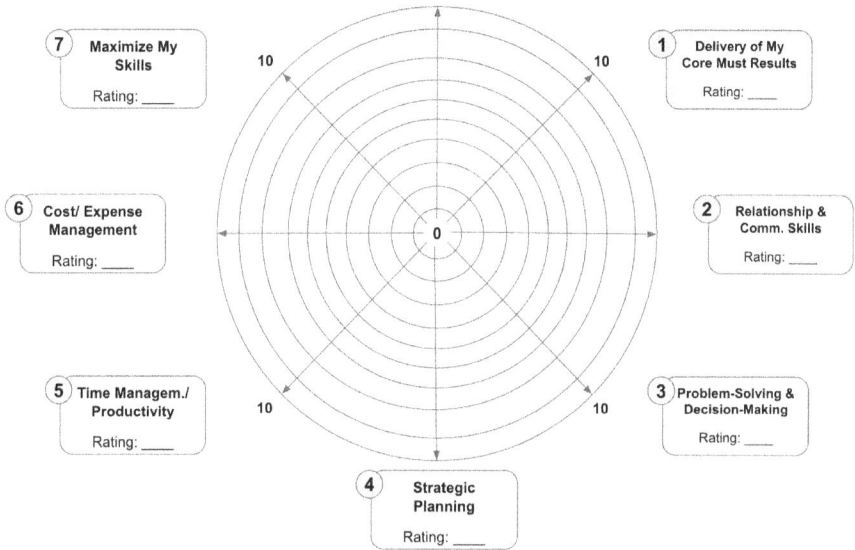

Exercise

1. Reflect on each area of your private and professional wheels of life. Write down briefly:
   - Your ultimate vision and standard
   - Where you are today
   - Where you came from (important because we always want to focus on our progress)
2. Rate the areas in your wheel of life on a scale of 0-10.

In addition to the outcome-based planning system, maintain organized documents and lists. Create one digital document for each category to capture all relevant notes. Keep a document for daily notes as well. Consider maintaining additional lists like "Someday/Maybe" and "Read/Review."

Fundamental 41: Use an outcome and purpose-based organization system to manage your life. Your system brings you clarity and mental space for focus—alongside innovation and progress.

4.12 Weekly and Daily Planning in your OPS

Reflecting on these principles as I write about them, I recently wondered why such fundamental concepts weren't taught in school. I thought about what might have been if I had started using them strategically 20 years ago. Well, maybe I would have missed some valuable lessons from learning the hard way and figuring things out myself—and I wouldn't be here now, writing this book and teaching this content. There are two lessons from this reflection: First, many things happen for a reason, and dots start connecting later on. Second, it makes sense to build on learnings and best practices. We can make a difference for ourselves and others, and it's never too late to start.

Many of my clients—and most people in general—are seeking more clarity and a stronger feeling of being in control. I understand this well because I've been there myself.

The key to clarity and control is doing the right things consistently. All of that is covered throughout this book. At this point, let's once again focus on the consistency piece—that gives us an answer to the question: How can we bring the OPS to life? It is through practicing daily and weekly planning as a consistent check-in point.

Weekly Planning Once per week, ideally on Sunday, set aside 1-2 hours. You only need your system, something to write with, and a clear mind (state of focus). Follow these steps:

1. Connect with what matters most—either generally or in each category—your purpose, vision, and outcomes.
2. Write down what needs to happen in each category to move forward—what will have the biggest impact and what are "musts."

3. Organize your to-dos from last week. Decide which ones still need to be done and moved to the next week.
4. Organize your week: schedule your "musts" into the calendar. Anticipate challenges and develop your strategy for success.
5. Finally—my favorite part—celebrate all victories from the last week, organized by your most important categories. Do it playfully and outrageously. Look forward to another amazing week ahead.

Daily Planning At day's end, review what you accomplished based on your plans. Determine if anything needs to move to the next day. Briefly review your actions for the week and see what else needs scheduling tomorrow. Ensure all musts are scheduled with sufficient buffer time between them.

I encourage you to do this in the evening. First, the planning takes some load off your mind and gives you more structure. As a consequence, you'll not only sleep better—you're directing your mind to anticipate what will be important and to prepare. When you wake up with clarity the next morning, you'll know exactly what to focus on first.

In the process of daily planning, also write any relevant notes into your (digital) daily note and reflection sheet, and write anything very personal and emotional into your journal, including your 3 wins or successes of the day. This is another way of conditioning your mind, and you can see it as a reward as it typically evokes positive feelings.

Fundamental 42: Practice weekly and daily planning consistently to stay connected with your priorities—in all areas of life that matter to you.

4.13 Multiply your Impact Beyond Yourself

The Power of Leveraging Actions

If we try to do everything by ourselves, we limit what we can achieve due to constraints of time, skill, and energy. To maximize our outcomes, it's crucial to discover the potential of delegating tasks to service providers or others.

Ask yourself: What tasks are you currently doing that aren't truly important for you to handle personally? Even for important tasks, could someone else potentially do them better? We call this "Leveraging" actions to another person. We choose this term instead of delegate or outsource because there's more to it than just getting rid of a task. Through leveraging, you're making things easier, creating a bigger impact, and building win-win situations.

There are two key dimensions to leveraging:

1. Others may simply be better at certain tasks and can create far superior results—particularly in areas outside your core skill set.
2. There are routine tasks that need to be done—tasks you might be good at and don't mind doing. However, when analyzed carefully, they don't significantly contribute to your desired outcomes.

The Value of Your Time

By leveraging tasks to others, you not only free up time for what's truly important—there's also a deeper emotional and spiritual dimension: you begin to value your time more. Consider the value of your time. While it's priceless in many ways as our scarcest resource, for this reflection, let's connect a concrete value with it.

Exercise: How much is your time worth?

> 1. *Calculate your number by considering: your hourly salary, years of experience, educational investments, opportunity costs (including time with loved ones) and the finite nature of time*
> 2. *What is your number?*
> 3. *Reflect and take action:*
>   > a. *What are activities which are neither meaningful to you, which definitely arenÄt worth your tie?value of tHow does this number change how you think about spending your time?*
>   > b. *Which specific activities will you leverage to others?*

Creating Win-Win Synergies

If money is a concern, think in terms of solutions. You could offer services in trade, such as tutoring someone in exchange for house cleaning.

Independently of this - consider how you and another person, or a group of people, can benefit from each other or how you can, by combining forces, create something much larger than the sum of the individual parts. I apply this in all of my professional relationships, whether it is in Bright Minds or at AWS. These relationships are built based on trust and shared values, genuine care as well as shared meaning (through purpose and vision). My teams, whether direct or virtual teams, know that there is growth in my proximity, and that I'll help them out if they need me - and equally I can rely on them. It's similar, by the way, with Mastermind groups, although we'll cover that in the next chapter.

Exercise:

1. *Reflect on your professional relationships:*
   - *Identify situations where you currently delegate tasks*
   - *Analyze cases where you truly leverage relationships and create mutual value*
2. *Explore potential new areas for leveraging:*
   - *Professional sphere: What additional tasks or responsibilities could you leverage?*
   - *Personal life: Which areas could benefit from strategic leveraging?*

Fundamental 43: Create greater impact by leveraging actions to others and collaborating—your time is your most precious resource. Create win-win situations, synergizing strengths with others.

4.14 Action Planning: Aligning Activities with Purpose and Vision

At the beginning of this chapter, we highlighted the controversy of managing to-dos first versus managing our life—and so we introduced the OPS life management system. The activity we refer to in this system is so much more than just the execution of to-dos. Also remember that language shapes our mindset and directs our focus—this is why we deliberately use the term "actions" rather than "to-dos."

Let's look more holistically at these actions. Every action happens for a reason and a purpose, yet in their busy lives, people often don't realize or focus on that. The problem then becomes doing activity without purpose and meaning—which is like taking the juice out of the way someone spends their life. This not only makes the process less enjoyable, it also prevents our brain from accessing its power to be creative and deliver top results.

Attaching Meaning and Outcomes to Our Actions

A more effective approach is to view actions holistically by connecting them to concrete purpose and vision. This enriched perspective enhances your mind's capabilities in several ways:

- Discovering new and more effective paths to your desired outcomes
- Structuring and combining similar activities more efficiently
- Prioritizing truly impactful activities
- Finding deeper meaning in everything you do

When we "chunk up" our thinking—grouping related actions into broader categories like body-related activities—we reduce perceived complexity. Instead of facing an overwhelming list of individual tasks, we can focus on investing time in meaningful categories. This approach makes it easier for our minds to process, store, and execute tasks effectively.

The simplest way to implement this method is through the outcome-based organization system you've already learned about.

The Action Planning Method

Another proactive way to apply these principles is outcome-based action planning. You can use it both as part of your OPS and independently as a planning tool for virtually any task—whether you're planning a product launch, a wedding, or structuring your day. This method, derived from Tony Robbins' RPM system, consists of three simple steps:

1. **Result**: Place your target in the center of the template. Make it specific and compelling. This is the outcome you're pursuing.
2. **Purpose**: Define the driving force that will give you energy to follow through. Ask yourself why you want to achieve this result, and use words that move you emotionally.
3. **Actions**: Brainstorm potential actions that could lead to your desired result. Select the most impactful ones, prioritize them, and list them in order on the left section of the sheet.

Beyond these core elements, you can enhance your plan by: Assigning priorities to each action, estimating duration, indicating which tasks can be leveraged, and marking essential tasks with asterisks (*). Below, you'll find a template to design your own outcome-based action plan. Remember: this isn't just a planning tool—it can fundamentally transform how you think about goals and achievement.

P	D	L	Massive Action Plan (MAP)	Result/ Outcome	Purpose
Musts					

Exercise: Create Your Outcome-Based Action Plan. Take a blank sheet of paper or use our template.

1. *Choose something that truly matters to you*
2. *Create an outcome-based action plan following the RPM method:*
   - *Define your specific Result (what you want to achieve)*
   - *Clarify your Purpose (why it matters to you)*
   - *List your Actions (how you'll make it happen)*
3. *Remember to mark priorities, estimate durations, and identify which tasks can be leveraged*

Fundamental 44: Use outcome-based action planning as your new default method and paradigm when you approach new outcomes. Another positive by-product is that you can elevate any activity from simple to-do to purposeful action.

4.15 Breaking Free from Stress

Many people believe stress is an inevitable companion to success. This is actually a myth and a belief that we should break—and extend our model of the world, because the "how" matters, and you've learned many success patterns for that already. When faced with growing business demands—more time, money, people—don't let opportunity become a source of stress. You have a choice about how you feel emotionally about these situations. Here are 3 principles for managing stress—or preventing it from occurring in the first place:

- **The Power of Three Options:** One source of stress in people's minds can be the perceived lack of options. This is why, as a coach, I often help clients see more alternatives or connect different parts. A simple yet helpful way to get out of stress, or avoid getting in, is to ensure you have at least 3 choices. As Tony Robbins notes in one of his recordings: "with one choice, you feel stressed; with two choices, you face a dilemma and still feel stressed. The solution? Always identify at least three options when making decisions. This simple shift creates emotional freedom."

- **Understanding Urgency:** We need to transform our belief system about urgency. Often, we get seduced by immediate completion—the satisfaction of getting something done right now. But frequently, these urgent matters don't truly matter. We're merely reacting to environmental demands. Remember: urgency is not your ally—it's the source of stress.

- **The Significance Trap:** People often fall into a pattern of making small things urgent and urgent things important. While this creates the illusion of a dynamic, powerful life, it actually generates unnecessary stress. The key is to honestly evaluate where you invest your time and energy.

Immediate Stress Relief Strategies

If you find yourself in a stressful situation, here are two simple steps you can take:

1. Direct your focus toward what you want, not what you fear
2. Question your perspective and reframe what situations mean to you

Consider this: two people can face the same experience with completely different interpretations. One might think "This is devastating," while another thinks "I can't wait to tackle this challenge and elevate my life to the next level." To release stress instantly, ask yourself questions such as:

- How will I feel about this in 10 years? Will it even matter?
- What's actually funny about this situation that I haven't noticed?

Often, people say they'll probably laugh about a stressful situation in 10 years. Why wait a decade? You can change your perspective in an instant. Shift your focus and reframe the meaning now—you don't need to wait a decade to see things differently.

Fundamental 45: Choose your emotional response to opportunity rather than defaulting to stress. When stuck in a decision dilemma, expand your perspectives—and remember, any situation offers at least three options for moving forward.

What we perceive as stress can often be an emotional signal from our subconscious that something is off—particularly when we're not using our time purposefully. The principle "Don't major in minor things" captures this perfectly.

As we already highlighted in the previous chapter when introducing the TimeMatrix, directing our time and energy to the most meaningful activities is crucial. That concept is great and as Stephen Covey suggests, it's helpful to make this "Q2-Thinking" part of your mindset. However, to really ensure that this sticks in our mind, there's another very helpful way to illustrate the concept, which immediately makes us realize what matters. This way of simplifying the concept again comes from Tony Robbins.

Time Targets: Win in the Game of Life

The "time targets" graphic makes it crystal clear: the greatest rewards come from activities at the center, while outer levels may still bring rewards but with diminishing fulfillment.

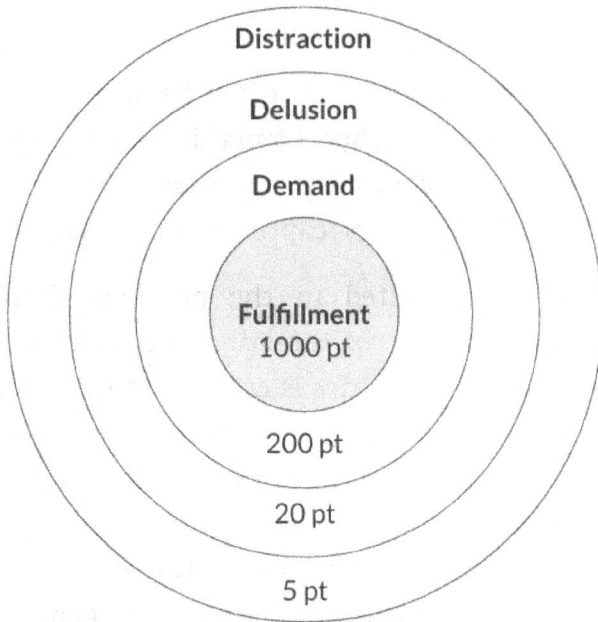

Let's just briefly recap the zones, which we introduced earlier.

- **The Fulfillment Zone (1000 Points):** Important but not urgent: health and exercise, spiritual time, connecting with nature, quality time with family and friends, planning, and skill development.
- **The Demand Zone (200 Points):** Important and urgent: Dealing with genuine "musts," not just "shoulds." Many achievers fall into the trap of spending too much time here, and this habit can become addictive. Our desire for significance often leads us to take on more, which builds capacity but risks neglecting what's truly important.
- **The Delusion Zone (20 Points):** Not important but urgent: responding to every phone call or email immediately. We delude ourselves into thinking these tasks must be done immediately and that we have no choice—but we do. A good strategy is to create specific time blocks for these

activities. Sometimes we welcome these as distractions, but they rarely create sustainable value.

- **The Distraction Zone (5 Points):** Not important and not urgent: spending hours watching Netflix or scrolling through Social Media. These activities provide momentary pleasure because they offer quick emotional relief when we're not truly fulfilled. While it's okay to spend some time here—everyone does—the question is how much. When you spend too much time in this zone, your subconscious likely sends you signals that something is off—do you recall any of these?

Maximizing Your Points and Reclaiming Your Time

The goal in the game of life is to maximize your points by spending significant time in the fulfillment zone. This positively affects all your relationships—simply because you treat others better when coming from a place of fulfillment rather than stress. The key to spending more time in the fulfillment zone? Connect with your categories of improvement and your deeper purpose. Purpose creates the drive to follow through.

By eliminating distracting activities, you automatically reclaim control of your time, potentially gaining several hours per day —time you can invest in something you love. Consider this: just one hour saved daily equals seven hours weekly—essentially a full workday. Imagine what you could learn or achieve with that time if you dedicated it to something you truly want to master. Or imagine the impact you could have if you used some of that time for your significant relationships.

Fundamental 46: Focus your time on activities that bring true fulfillment, which is the center of your time target—rather than getting caught in the outer rings of distraction and delusion.

4.17 Maximizing Your Impact Through Focus: 12 Principles for Focus and Flow

We've covered different concepts to maximize the impact of what you do so far in this chapter. With all that in place, the following chapter makes you even achieve beyond that. We will explore how you can get into a state of deep work and flow more consistently. The following best practices are inspired from the work done by Mihaly Csikszentmihalyi and Cal Newport, and enriched by experiences from my own professional and coaching practice.

Why is Focused Work so Important?

Creating something new, learning and mastering skills, and achieving outstanding results require us to be in a specific state —similar to chemistry, where certain temperatures are needed for desired reactions. We'll call this a flow state, and what we mean by that is any state of strong focus and deep work—when we're involved in an activity so deeply that nothing else seems to matter and we are creating "10X results" (the latter term inspired by the books from Grant Cardone and Dan Sullivan).

We'll concentrate here on 12 principles to get into states of deep focus and flow. There is a great opportunity in learning these concepts to create greater impact. But there's also a great urgency and importance to apply them consciously, because today's world can be so distracting.

Setting the Context

Before diving into the 12 principles, consider three key factors:

    1. The *Why* matters—you achieve the highest yields

when your focused activity aligns with your career and purpose.

2. Engage all your intelligences in deep focused work to maximize learning. For example, leverage emotions to enhance learning and embody the experience.

3. Iterate between different focused states, including execution, imagination, creation, connection, and inspiration.

We've organized these principles into four categories: time-related, environment-related, distraction-management, and mindset & brain-related practices.

Key Principles of Deep Focus and Flow

Time Management

1. **Schedule time for deeply focused work** and treat these blocks as "musts." A best practice is to schedule a fixed time window during the day and longer blocks on specific days of the week.

2. **Schedule time blocks for potentially distracting activities** such as internet browsing, phone use, and social media. When engaging spontaneously, remain conscious of what you're doing and keep your overall plans and timing in mind. Focus on the "big rocks" rather than managing "clutter" and trying to squeeze every little task into your calendar, as Stephen Covey suggests in his metaphor.

3. Set **ambitious deadlines** that will force you to concentrate at the limit of your ability. Estimate the time you need, then cut it down drastically.

Fundamental 47: Schedule dedicated blocks for focused work. Treat them as non-negotiable commitments, and create ambitious deadlines—while consciously containing potential distractions to specific times.

Managing Environment

1. **Create a deep focus location:** Define a space dedicated exclusively to deep work, such as a conference room, library, or home office. This becomes your sanctuary for focused, undistracted work—a zone where you can be "in the zone." If space is limited, at minimum ensure you have a proper table or desk for working.
2. **Design a deep focus environment:** Make your chosen space distraction-free and well-equipped with necessary tools and resources. This includes maintaining a clean desk, having sufficient water, keeping your notebook within reach, and your phone at a distance.

Fundamental 48: Create and design dedicated spaces for deep work. Equip them with the essential tools while eliminating potential distractions—and make them your sanctuary for focus and flow states.

Managing Distractions

1. **Email:** Keep the volume of emails low and create an environment/culture that promotes clear standards. Emails should include the current state, ultimate goal, and next steps. This helps close mental loops and avoid unnecessary back-and-forth.
2. **Social Media:** Take time consciously to respond to messages or check news feeds. Turn off notifications to prevent messages from creating open loops in your mind. Give yourself at least one day per week completely free from social media.
3. **Constantly reduce and eliminate shallow work:** Create an outcome-focused culture around you. When

someone asks you to do a shallow task, ask about the desired outcome—often you can help them understand the action isn't necessary, as there's likely a more effective solution. Practice saying "no" to shallow work tasks. However, make exceptions when someone sincerely asks for a favor that matters deeply to them. These relationship-building actions come from the heart—making them meaningful after all.

Fundamental 49: reate a context and culture for deep focus: actively manage/prevent potential interruptions (e.g. email, social media), set clear communication standards, and say "no" to unnecessary shallow work.

Mindset & Execution

1. **Train your ability to focus:** You can do this through regular meditation or by letting your brain experience low-stimuli moments. For example, when waiting for a friend outside a bar, consciously resist checking your phone.
2. **Create clear links between focus time and outcomes:** Define specific metrics of success for your focus time blocks, keep them visible, and measure results. Metrics might include completing a presentation, writing a 500-word article, or creating a strategy.
3. **Create accountability:** First and foremost, be accountable to yourself—analyzing your outcomes during weekly and daily planning is an excellent way to do this. Additionally, choose one or more accountability partners.

Fundamental 50: Strengthen your "focus muscle" through deliberate practice of low-stimuli moments and focus. Link your focus time to measurable outcomes, and create systems for measurement and accountability.

Celebration and Recharging

And finally, celebrate what you've achieved in your focused time. Give yourself the gift of feeling pride and gratitude for your achievements, to disconnect and recharge. You can do this throughout the day by consciously enjoying your breaks—through conversation, meditation, reading, an espresso, a walk, workout, or enjoying nature.

Another way to celebrate your achievements is to perform a workday shutdown ritual. This could be part of your daily planning: reflect on the day's achievements, note what remains unfinished and important, schedule and anticipate the next day, and finally say "All done!" This creates an anchor to switch from one state to another. You can emphasize the effect through the TRIAD by engaging your physical body as well—for example, doing 10 pushups.

Fundamental 51: Distinguish your deep work state by flipping an imaginary switch—or even combine this with a ritual. When you are done with deep work states, honor your achievements with conscious celebration and recharging activities.

Exercise: *Reflection*
1. *Go through the 12 principles. To what extent have you already implemented them or not?*
2. *Consider the potential impact of these principles on your situation and why adopting them more fully would benefit you*
3. *Select two or three principles you want to implement, and outline specific next steps for incorporating them into your routine*

4.18 Taking Care of Your Physical Body

Last but not least, let's explore how we can maximize our impact through our physical body. Our body is the center of our health, longevity, vitality and physical power—and one of the keys for mental clarity. Our body carries us through life, and not just us —when we do well, we can use that expanding vitality, power and clarity to love and to contribute. According to Buddhism, the body is a mandala, a holy temple, and naturally sacred. Let's be grateful to nature for the gift of life, and commit to treat our body for the miracle that it is, treat it like a temple.

Therein lies a very significant lever to creating impact. And while it's a lever that can be improved—on the other end of the spectrum, there's the potential to lose life if we don't take care of our body well.

Five Undeniable Truths About Health and Vitality

The best practices you will read in this section are meant as inspiration—pick the ones that work for you. I realize that for some people, the ability to eat what they want, whenever they want, seems to be a religious thing. So these best practices might not be for everyone; however, as you picked up this book, it is likely that many of the tips will resonate with you.

While each body is unique, there are undeniable truths about what benefits and harms our bodies. The first step is to accept these truths. Then making these changes requires the right mindset, purpose, habits, systems, and accountability—which is all covered in this book. Here are five undeniable truths:

1. When people snack, they rarely do it from hunger— most often they're trying to fulfill an emotional need.

2. People usually get tired not because they're sleepy, but because they eat poorly.
3. To maximize your chances of living a vital, long life, you must do both: eat healthily and exercise —practicing one and ignoring the other is not sustainable.
4. Our body has self-healing capabilities, which we can either empower or inhibit through our lifestyle choices and daily habits.
5. Poor sleep habits can undermine even the best nutrition and exercise routines. The quality of sleep matters at least as much as the quantity.

My Personal Health Journey

I have personally tried different forms of nutrition—in most cases to optimize health, energy, and vitality; and sometimes simply out of curiosity. For example, I've used a glucose sensor in my arm that is connected to an app, to measure how lifestyle and food affect my insulin levels. I learned that through the right sequence and composition of food, my blood sugar level remains mostly flat. This not just positively affects my energy and focus —it also contributes to longevity.

I did several experiments, testing good practices but also negative ones—since this is such an immersive way for learning. For example, I deliberately drank half liter of Coca-Cola and ate a Kinder Bueno on an empty stomach. I could see in the data that my insulin rose from 90 to 200 and then dropped to 60, all within less than an hour. And my emotions and physical state? I felt excited and restless with an increased pulse as my blood sugar level shot up; and then tired, and starving for more sugar when it was down, and slowly normalizing again. It is so interesting what effect food has on our body system. And what I call an experiment is an everyday habit for some people.

I also had many more subtle and less obvious insights. For example, about the order and composition of my healthy shake that I have daily in the afternoon. When I eat the banana 30 minutes later, instead of mixing it into the shake, it causes a much lower spike—this helps me to maintain my energy in the afternoon.

Other experiments included fasting for 6 days, or keto for three weeks. Besides the effects on my body, I also closely observed the impact on my mindset and energy. It is also always a great opportunity to practice discipline and willpower; and to grow personally.

Mindset as Source of Physical Transformation

My coaching and SUCCESS HABITS clients similarly have major insights and go through substantial transformations when they work on their body—changing their exercise and nutrition habits.

One example is my client Max. As we did a water-only fasting challenge, Max surpassed everyone else resisting food for eight entire days. He lost 5 kg during that week and maintained the discipline and willpower—which made him lose another 7 kg over the following months. He developed consistent nutrition and exercise habits, which complement well his other success habits. This led him to strive in other areas of his life as well, including personal relationships—and a major career jump that he did recently. For context: Max has been an achiever already, but we could yet unlock a next level within him. As a classic example, through overcoming inner obstacles, connecting with higher vision and purpose; setting goals and taking right actions consistently.

Your Body Is Your Responsibility

The intent of the best practices shared here is inspiring you to live a healthier and more vital life. No matter if you're moving from unhealthy to healthy; or if you are already very healthy and vital, and want to unlock your next level. Pick up the information that serves you and decide what's right for you. Keep in mind: your body is your responsibility, and you have a choice. Many people complain about conflicting food advice, but remember: successful people don't complain—they take responsibility and act. Ultimately, health affects not only ourselves but also our ability to contribute to our loved ones.

Fundamental 52: Your body is your ultimate asset—treat it like a sacred temple through disciplined nutrition, movement, and rest. Your physical vitality determines your capacity to serve and create impact.

4.19 Nurturing the Four Dimensions, Including Nutrition

Here are my personal fundamentals about food, nutrition, physical exercise, and nurturing mind and spirit. These derive from one of my highest values: treating the body well. Note: This is not nutrition advice—consult with a nutrition specialist or doctor when in doubt.

Food and Nutrition

1. Eat lots of greens. Include an abundance of salad and herbs.
2. Eat "living" foods as much as possible, such as vegetables and nuts (rather than processed food).
3. Practice intermittent fasting: define eating windows and ideally reduce your feeding time to 8 hours or less. Personally, I follow 16:8 intermittent fasting, eating typically between 12-7 PM.
4. Fast for 24 hours once per week. I choose Sundays for this.
5. Define your fundamental foods that provide nutrients.
6. Avoid nutrient-poor carbs such as white noodles, rice, and white bread.
7. Maintain a mostly vegan diet. Personally, my only animal products are fish (2-3 times per week), organic meat (once per month), and eggs (1-2 times per week).
8. Choose olive oil over sunflower or rapeseed oil. Coconut oil is also a good option.
9. Eliminate sugar. Be cautious with fruit sugar and reduce/avoid juices. Extracting juice from fruits is not the natural way of consuming them—you'll see this in blood sugar levels after drinking a glass.
10. Eat in a specific order to keep blood glucose levels stable: start with salad, then proteins and fats, then

carbs. Always choose slow carbs such as lentils or beans.

11. Minimize or eliminate alcohol consumption.
12. Drink plenty of water. Drink two glasses of warm water first thing after waking up.

FUNDAMENTAL 53: Nourish your body with living foods, strategic meal timing, and mindful consumption. Your nutrition choices shape your daily energy and long-term vitality.

Physical Exercise

- **Morning activation:** Activate your body every morning first thing with movement. I do this for 5-6 minutes with pushups, situps, supermans and squats. I mix in some stretching and the down dog yoga pose as well.
- **Exercise:** At least 4 times exercise per week, including: 2 times over 35 minutes a workout that activates your cardiovascular system; and 2 times weight workout for at least 20 minutes.

FUNDAMENTAL 54: Ultimate physical power requires daily activation. Start each morning with movement for at least 5-10 minutes. Practice regular cardio and strength training, at least 3-4 times per week.

Engaging Mind and Spirit as well

Meditate daily. There are many forms of meditation, offering flexibility in your approach. Reading Tim Ferriss' "Tools of Titans," I noted that nearly all 101 high-performing people interviewed share one habit—they meditate. You can follow guided meditations from apps, Spotify, or YouTube. I often use the 6-Step meditation by Vishen Lakhiani, Tony Robbins' daily priming, and Joe Dispenza's meditations. Ideally, take 15-30 minutes for meditation. If that doesn't fit into your day, dedicate at least 5 minutes to conscious stillness.

Additionally, take small meditative moments throughout the day. For example, pause for a moment, smile, and take 3 conscious deep breaths. You might feel like yawning when you do this—embrace it and give yourself a little hug.

FUNDAMENTAL 55: Cultivate inner stillness through daily meditation—it's a #1 practice shared by high achievers. Meditation brings mental clarity, spiritual power, and lets you connect with your intuition to treat your body well.

Exercise: Review these best practices and select 3-5 areas that will make the biggest impact on your wellbeing. Then commit to specific actions for consistent implementation.

PHASE 5: LEADERSHIP, DISCIPLINE AND ACCOUNTABILITY

Chapter 5 explores what it means to lead yourself effectively, maintain discipline, embrace accountability, and show up fully —both to yourself and others. We'll also examine decision-making, responsibility, and ultimately, how to create an environment where you can thrive.

5.1 Growth Requires Your Initiative

The principles outlined in this book are fundamental life skills that work across all areas of success. Yet remarkably, these critical tools for personal mastery are rarely taught in traditional education. While a complete discussion of our education system would fill an entire book, the essential point is this: the responsibility for your personal growth rests in your own hands. Growth is not a passive achievement – it requires conscious effort, deliberate practice, and unwavering commitment to your own development.

Pressure Is a Good Thing

Through my communities and various professional development programs, I've met hundreds of people exploring Personal Development, Leadership, Neuro-Linguistic Programming, Effectiveness, Hypnosis, and related fields. Some are coaches looking to expand their skill set to better serve their clients. Many others attend these trainings simply for their own personal growth.

As I've observed, people typically come to this work during one of three life phases. As humans constantly evolving, we're likely all experiencing one of these phases—or if not currently, we've been there before and will likely encounter them again:

1. Experiencing intense pressure or pain
2. Already living at their edge and seeking the next level
3. Feeling neutral but searching for more meaning, purpose, and vision—sensing that something's missing

While these situations differ, they share one common element:

pressure. Pressure is simply an emotion—and while its causes can vary, ultimately it's something we create in our minds.

Fundamental 56: Embrace pressure as a catalyst for growth. Pressure is not something to avoid, but rather a self-created emotion that signals an opportunity for breakthrough and personal evolution.

5.2 The Choice to Break Through

I believe success is determined by how we act under pressure. These pivotal moments can lead to either breakthrough—discovery, insight, and growth—or escape. Breakthrough means facing challenges, even when uncomfortable. It means leaving your comfort zone or, as Tony Robbins says, "slaying those dragons" to reach your next level.

What does escape look like? When things get uncomfortable, we might distract ourselves by watching Netflix or scrolling through social feeds; numb ourselves with excessive eating or alcohol; or even pursue seemingly positive hobbies excessively—all to avoid what truly needs to be done.

What determines our response to pressure? What makes the difference between breakthrough and escape? Two main factors come into play: willpower, which encompasses your mindset, and environment. We'll cover environment at the end of this chapter, but here's a preview: your environment is, in most cases, something you can choose. While success is largely our own mental game, we can make it exponentially easier through a supportive peer group and environment. Both willpower and environment are crucial, but environment typically proves stronger—which is why it's so important to consciously choose and design it.

Mindset is crucial. Everything we've covered so far matters—including mindset mastery and design, vision and purpose, strong habits, effective prioritization, outcome-based organization, and energy and focus management. While these tools will take you far, there will be moments of intense pressure. How can you ensure that in these moments, you don't escape and let these powerful tools evaporate? This is where Self-Leadership, Discipline, and Accountability come in.

Exercise for self-reflection. Think of examples from your own life history, and reflect about them.

1. *A period when you experienced pressure, where you did a breakthrough. What made the difference, to make you break through? What changed in your next level?*
2. *A period when you experienced pressure, when you bounced back. What made you stay in the comfort zone? What did you learn from it?*

Fundamental 57: In moments of pressure, choose breakthrough rather than escape. Decide if this is a worthwhile challenge and then, first and foremost, face it. Be prepared to persist through whatever obstacles may come—supported by your willpower and a positive environment including your peer group.

5.3 Case Study: Discipline is the Glue that Makes You Follow Through

Consider my client Anna (name changed), whose story perfectly illustrates these principles. Through our coaching sessions, she overcame significant emotional challenges rooted in her childhood. This freed her mind in many ways, allowing her to focus again on her wants, next steps, and long-term vision. Her medium-term dream was to secure a position at her dream company.

Anna went through all five phases of Success Habits. She was an exemplary client who did herself a favor by truly implementing what she discovered and learned. What stood out was her exceptional discipline and accountability—both to herself and to me as her coach.

She committed to daily fundamentals—workout, affirmations, visualization, power poses—disciplining herself to maintain positive focus until it became natural. In her job search, she sent out applications, followed up diligently, and invested genuine effort. When her dream job opportunity arose two months into our coaching, she was more than ready—not just through the coaching, but through what she made of it.

During the application phase at one of the top companies in her industry, Anna showed up as her authentic self. She connected deeply with the team during a dinner meeting and engaged meaningfully with her potential hiring manager, discussing industry vision and purpose. These weren't just interview questions—they came from her heart. Because she had done the inner work and connected deeply with her own vision and purpose, she naturally fostered an inspiring connection with the woman who would become her manager in the job she now loves.

Fundamental 58: Discipline is the bridge between insight and achievement—commit daily to your fundamentals until they become natural. This allows your authentic self to emerge and your vision to materialize.

5.4 Leadership is the Starting Point for Each Transformation

At the beginning of any transformation is leadership. Whether it is Martin Luther King, Nelson Mandela, or Mother Teresa—who changed the mindset of millions and transformed entire nations —or whether it is you leading yourself: showing up, working on your mindset, doing all the things you've learned in this book. At the end of the day, the principle is similar: there must be a leader. You must be able to lead yourself first; lead others to enhance your impact; and of course allow others to lead you—those who serve you and act in the interest of everyone's greater good.

What is leadership actually? In business practice, let's look at the definition by Peter Drucker: "Leadership is lifting a person's vision to high sights, the raising of a person's performance to a higher standard, the building of a personality beyond its normal limitations." Drucker also emphasizes that leadership is about having followers, doing the right things, and creating results. I would argue that each of us is or can be a leader to others—as we lead and inspire others in our unique way: whether we are following our personal or professional vision and purpose. Of course with different "flavors" and dimensions of impact. In the *Success Habits Program*, we dedicate a larger sub-chapter about leadership in organizations.

Leading Yourself Requires you to Control Your Emotions

Let's also look at the definition of Leadership by Tony Robbins, as it fits very well into our personal development context (note that he also uses the same principles and definitions in his businesses). "Leadership is the ability to significantly influence the thoughts, feelings, actions, and behaviors of those you lead." But in order to do this with someone else, in the very first instance, good leaders must manage themselves: this means controlling their own thoughts, feelings, actions, and behaviors.

Self-leadership is the enabler for discipline, as discipline demands control of our emotions and resistance to momentary urges. Consequently, mastering our emotions is needed—and that is the ability to consistently shift from any unbeneficial state to a resourceful state instantaneously. This is what self-leadership is about at its core.

Fundamental 59: Self-leadership is fundamental for your own discipline and for leading others—your ability to control your own emotions, thoughts, and behaviors is the foundation for creating meaningful transformation, whether personal or collective.

5.5 Discipline Brings Freedom

The Freedom Paradox

This headline might seem contradictory to common sense, which often equates freedom with the absence of boundaries and giving in to momentary desires. Many people today would say that freedom means letting go and doing nothing, or eating whatever they crave. However, boundaries are necessary. Our human body naturally tends to preserve energy, choose the path of least resistance, seek short-term pleasure, and avoid any kind of immediate pain.

These energy-preserving tendencies were crucial for survival for centuries. In modern societies, we have instant access to food, and when we use all our power, for example in a workout, we remain safe—there's no mammoth going to hunt us. While these energy-preserving tendencies should be outdated nowadays, they often remain ingrained in us. We must be aware that these triggers still exist and, more importantly, that they can be exploited. Consider how corporations promote euphemistic foods, stimulating entertainment, social media feeds, and other energy-preserving activities that guarantee instant short-term pleasure. Of course, other "urges" are triggered here as well, like the need for variety, connection, and love.

People "freely" consume what they crave, which is hard to resist. But consider this—when struggling against urges triggered by emotionally designed addictive content, how free are they really? Unrestrained behavior, which serves neither personal growth nor the greater good, is generally the opposite of freedom.

Why We Need to Own and Protect Our Freedom

If freedom means the opposite of unrestrainedness—if it means choosing consciously rather than being controlled by externally evoked emotions—how can we achieve more of it? You already know the answer—there are different levers which we introduced throughout the book. The key is that you must be proactive about it, for two main reasons.

First, many businesses make money by triggering people's momentary urges. Here are just a few examples:

- The food industry promotes the midday crash after a burger and fries as something fun and normal
- The entertainment industry validates endless streaming as "quality time," without questioning what hours of daily series watching does to their users
- Social media companies exploit our needs for belonging, love, and connection by evoking emotions that keep us scrolling through their feeds

Second, broader society and common sense rarely question these patterns—quite the opposite. Promoting discipline as a vehicle for freedom potentially challenges many people's identity, beliefs and lifestyle choices—including their definition of what "freedom" means. Many people still connect freedom mainly with letting go, and doing what comes to mind. And isn't freedom such a substantial value? When you challenge this, you can see where this could lead.

This is why my perspective and recommendation is: do not try to convince others proactively—but rather show up as a role model when it comes to discipline. If you do this congruently, you will soon realize how you extend people's model of reality. And with this, we can slowly and step by step spread the worldview that discipline actually brings freedom.

Discipline in its Simplest Form: Just Do It

In the next sections, we will explore more deeply what discipline is, what it is beneficial for and how we can be more disciplined. Before doing that and getting more scientific about it, let's break it down to the basics. Discipline comes down to using our minds and training ourselves to choose consciously in each moment. Discipline means to **just do it**, whether you feel like it or not.

Want to transform your body? Exercise consistently and maintain proper nutrition. Seeking career advancement? Strategically invest in your skills and relationships beyond what others are willing to do. Looking for meaningful partnership? Cultivate your best self and create opportunities for connection through deliberate action.

This straightforward approach sets the foundation for our deeper exploration of discipline and its powerful companion, accountability.

Exercise:

1. *Reflect on examples from your life where discipline has led to greater freedom.*
2. *Identify areas in your life where you could apply more of a "just do it" attitude.*

Fundamental 60: Embrace discipline as the path to true freedom. Master your impulses rather than being mastered by them so you can shape your destiny. The secret formula to overcoming struggle and resistance? "Just do it!"

5.6 What Discipline is and Why it Matters

Let's look more closely at discipline and why it matters. Discipline is the ability to restrain immediate impulses in pursuit of what truly serves you. When you're disciplined, you act with intention and maintain complete control over your choices. Discipline means choosing long-term fulfillment over instant gratification.

Why does it matter so much? When we are disciplined, we moderate ourselves based on our values and avoid excess. This becomes especially crucial as success and wealth provide us with the means to pursue unlimited desires. Whether it's new projects and opportunities, indulgent foods, romantic relationships, fitness pursuits, or even travel—balancing these requires clarity and discipline. This heightened consciousness leads to a **better life**. Instead of letting uncontrolled emotions drive your actions, you develop deeper self-awareness and intentional choice.

Ultimately, this is what gives you **true freedom**—the power to choose in every moment what truly matters to you. This freedom extends into the dimension of time as well. For example, having the discipline to rise early when your alarm sounds gives you the freedom to shape your day according to your priorities and fit in everything that matters to you.

5.7 Discipline to Navigate Better through Life

Discipline Helps You Get Through Hard Times

Life inevitably brings moments of pain. While we can anticipate and minimize negative experiences, the truth is—if we choose to live life to the fullest by growing, breaking barriers, and stepping out of our comfort zone into bigger versions of ourselves—we will face challenging situations. These challenges and obstacles are actually opportunities to learn and grow. Whether an ambitious project falls short of expectations and requires a fresh start, someone gives you difficult feedback or rejection, treats you unfairly, or you fall short of your own standards—hard times will emerge as we pursue a life of meaning.

So how do we prepare? Anticipation and preparation are key. And developing the consistent preparation needed for all obstacles and opportunities requires discipline. Expect that you may get punched in the mouth from time to time, metaphorically or even physically. However, through discipline, you create your own zone of stability—one you can return to through your success habits: a zone of clarity, focus, and certainty. With that certainty, you continue to step up and move forward, knowing that the bigger reward lies ahead. You understand that whatever happens contains truth and learning that will help you master the next opportunity—after all, that's how we grow.

Think about the last time you received negative feedback or rejection. How you handled those emotions is something we explored in the first chapter. But the key point here is that when you've established success habits through discipline, you have your zone. And in that zone, you can always access resilience and resourcefulness.

Fundamental 61: Discipline is an anchor that gives you resilience, even when your environment and markets get stormy. Discipline yourself to practice your habits and master your state. This will make you invincible, and being in that state, you can tackle challenges as opportunities, while others are stuck.

Discipline Helps You Maintain Success in Good Times

As your success grows, it becomes crucial to keep your ego in check. Discipline yourself not to brag. While you can be proud and celebrate achievements—as a great leader, you'll likely moderate your celebration, knowing the market never sleeps and new challenges lie ahead. Your success might indicate higher standards than others—but remember, competition never rests, and your partners' expectations continue to rise. You're now a role model, which brings great responsibility. Remember: don't feel or behave in a superior way. Instead, focus on reaching your next level by concentrating on what you can influence. Being a leader means understanding what may have stopped others and finding ways to help them achieve results. Often, we can accomplish this by asking the right questions from a state of genuine connection and rapport.

Don't let success lead to self-destructive behavior. This might mean making substantial money then squandering it on unnecessary purchases. Or celebrating a promotion by drinking excessively, sacrificing not only brain cells but also reputation. Or achieving a significant breakthrough with your client but failing to follow through consistently, letting the value evaporate for both parties. Discipline helps you maintain a sharp mindset and winner mentality through all circumstances.

Fundamental 62: Maintain discipline in moments of victory. Celebration and rewarding yourself are great, however only to an extent. Your commitment to staying sharp and humble during success determines your long-term impact.

Discipline Helps you to Handle Pleasure

As you apply success habits consistently, life becomes more exciting and filled with pleasure. However, don't fall into the trap of constantly seeking pleasure. Instead, consciously create and choose moments of contrast—empowering ones. You can practice this by deliberately putting yourself into challenging situations, such as taking an ice bath or completing an intense workout. Regularly experiencing discomfort not only builds resilience—it also enhances your ability to appreciate and savor life's pleasant moments more deeply.

Fundamental 63: Consciously embrace discomfort to enhance life's pleasures—your willingness to seek out challenging experiences like intense workouts or ice baths builds resilience and deepens your appreciation for life's rewards.

Discipline Helps You Handle Power

With discipline comes success, and you're likely to gain or take on more responsibility—and power. The most self-disciplined individuals maintain control over themselves; as a result, they don't seek control over others, although they naturally command significant influence. Power means control, impact, and leverage—all desirable outcomes when handled consciously for good. Never fall into the trap of abusing power—discipline is essential here too. Whatever need you seek to fulfill (relating back to Chapter 1), through discipline, you can always find a healthy way to meet that need with certainty.

When power emerges from self-control, it's natural that great leaders often prioritize their subordinates' needs above their own, particularly regarding short-term rewards and pleasure. The leader, guided by vision, mission, and determination to follow through, keeps the longer-term objective in mind and trusts the process.

Fundamental 64: Use your power (which means your control, impact, and leverage over others) consciously and for good. Continue to serve, and discipline yourself to never abuse power. You can use your own mantra, such as "Leaders eat last".

5.8 Accountability: Taking Full Ownership of Results

Accountability is taking complete responsibility for both your actions and your outcomes. It goes beyond simply being responsible—it means owning not just what you do, but also what you don't do, and most importantly, the results you achieve or fail to achieve.

Connecting Accountability Back to Discipline Discipline is the product of your mindset-related factors, including willpower and your environment including systems. It is the ability to consistently take action and maintain standards despite momentary urges or distractions. **Accountability** creates the context and framework; it can be expressed in terms of expectations and KPIs. They work together in a powerful cycle:

How Accountability Strengthens Discipline:

- Creates clear expectations and standards to measure against
- Provides external motivation when internal motivation wavers
- Makes progress (or lack thereof) visible and undeniable
- Adds consequences to our actions or inactions
- Forces us to confront reality rather than rationalize

How Discipline Enables Accountability:

- Builds the daily habits needed to meet commitments
- Develops the mental toughness to face difficult truths
- Creates consistent actions that can be tracked and measured
- Establishes a track record of reliability
- Maintains focus on long-term outcomes over short-term

comfort

To summarize, they create a virtuous cycle: accountability provides the structure and motivation that strengthens discipline, while discipline provides the consistent action that makes accountability meaningful. Neither is as effective without the other—discipline without accountability can drift off course, while accountability without discipline lacks the follow-through to create real change.

Fundamental 65: Through accountability, create a context and framework for your discipline. This will make it much easier to maintain your discipline, and provide ways to measure it. Together they create unstoppable momentum: accountability strengthens discipline, while discipline fulfills accountability.

5.9 How to Practice Discipline and Accountability

After covering what discipline is, why it matters, and how it benefits us—as well as introducing accountability—here are 7 practical tips to increase your discipline:

1. **Be clear about your purpose.** This will help you show up, even when you don't feel like it. These are actually the moments of greatest victory.
2. **Make it a must.** Make your commitment non-negotiable. Turn "should" into "must." When something becomes a must, you find a way to make it happen no matter what.
3. **Build your mindset foundation.** Your map of the world—including your identity, beliefs, and values—forms important fundamentals that can be either enablers or showstoppers.
4. **Prioritize your purpose.** Do first things first, planning and organizing consciously. Yes, keeping your house clean and orderly matters, but what matters most right now?
5. **Prepare your environment and body.** This relates to what you learned in the previous chapter. Being disciplined means making the right decisions consistently. For your body, that requires maintaining an optimal state—through eating well, exercising regularly, getting enough rest, and sleeping well. For your environment, consider all dimensions—including who you spend time with and where you choose to be.
6. **Remember nuances matter.** Prioritize constant improvement over perfectionism. Timing matters too. Sometimes you must relentlessly pursue goals, push yourself, and hold others accountable. Other times,

waiting makes sense. Avoid black-and-white thinking —be proactive and strategic about applying your willpower.

7. **Create systems for discipline:**
   - System for Habits: Create a reliable framework that makes success repeatable
   - System for Accountability: Use tools to measure actions and progress
   - Accountability Partners: Engage coaches, mentors, or friends

Remember: sporadic excellence is far less powerful than consistent good performance. It's not what you do occasionally that shapes your life—it's what you do consistently.

Exercise:

1. *Rate yourself on each of the seven best practices, using a scale of 1-10.*
2. *Write one reflection sentence for each rating and define one action per category.*
3. *Plan your accountability system:*
   - *Choose one habit for self-accountability*
   - *Select one tracking tool*
   - *Identify at least one accountability partner*

Fundamental 66: Follow the 7 Steps for enhancing discipline: Clarity about Purpose, Make it a Must, Mindset Foundation, Purpose Priority, Context (environment and body), Constant Improvement, and Systems for Discipline.

5.10 Taking Powerful Decisions

The decisions you take largely determine the outcomes you get in life. So the quality of your decisions is crucial, yet decision-taking is something we never really learned. At the same time, the spectrum of options and potential paths is huge and continuously increasing. As a consequence, many people struggle with decision-making, either through analysis paralysis or by making snap judgments without proper consideration. Let's explore a systematic approach to making decisions that serve your highest good.

Start with the Outcome

In the very first instance, always start with the outcome. What is it that you want ultimately? And is this a must or just a nice-to-have, could you de-prioritize or drop it entirely? When you truly connect with that desired outcome, the answer often arises naturally. When you decide to do something, also think of what you would have to de-prioritize or drop in favor of it. When you do that, for a lot of the simpler decisions, the answer is often very obvious.

For more complex decisions, follow these seven steps of our 7-Steps Decision Framework which is inspired by Tony Robbins:

1. **Define your Outcome:** Distinguish between "must-haves" and "nice-to-haves"
2. **Generate Options:** Identify different paths to reach your outcome
3. **Evaluate Consequences:** Assess the impact of each option
4. **Create Alternatives:** Look for win-win scenarios and creative solutions that might maximize outcomes—

often this step reveals new possibilities

5. **Validate Options:** Research and gather missing information. Seek advice from carefully chosen mentors or experts once you've clarified your best options

6. **Relax and Allow Integration:** Once your options are clear, give yourself time to process. Take a walk, work out, or do something different—let your unconscious mind work on the decision

7. **Decide and Act:** Once you make the decision, act immediately

Maintaining Flexibility

Following this process for the big decisions can greatly increase the quality of your decisions and outcomes. After taking a decision, of course start executing right away—nevertheless, also remain flexible to re-evaluate when new information or unconscious signals occur. Changing course when appropriate is part of the natural success cycle—it's not about being right initially, but about constantly adjusting one's course.

Common Decision Traps to Avoid

- Making decisions from a place of fear rather than opportunity
- Letting others' urgency become your emergency
- Overvaluing short-term comfort over long-term benefit
- Failing to consider the cost of inaction

Focus on the Outcome and Not Perfectionism

The goal isn't about being right, or making perfect decisions. Instead, it is about making decisions and then moving— and making them perfect through your commitment to the outcome. The goal is always the outcome. And the way we get there is part of the outcome as well—but that's not about perfection.

Exercise: *Applying the 7-Steps Decision Framework*

1. *Think about a decision in your life or work that you've been postponing.*
2. *Apply the 7-Steps Framework to this decision.*

Fundamental 67: Make decisions based on desired outcomes rather than current circumstances and avoidance. Generate options, evaluate consequences, validate options, relax and integrate, decide and act. Move quickly whenever you can, and remain flexible to adjust course when new information emerges.

5.11 Our Unconscious Mind as Guide for Decisions

Do you know that feeling when something is on your chest, or on your mind—when you know something isn't right? Often this signals that you need to make a decision, to change something from the status quo. Then the question arises: how to act on that signal? Change your environment? Your blueprint? Or your mindset?

The most successful leaders don't necessarily have the most information; they have great intuition for decision-making. They trust their "gut" feeling. This won't always lead to the right outcome, but it does more often than not—which is how they constantly grow as people of influence by being right frequently. Does this mean we can't be successful without a strong connection to intuition? Of course it's possible, but it'll be much harder. And others will notice—consciously or unconsciously—when someone is fighting hard rather than flowing naturally. So having a good connection with our intuition matters.

My Journey to Better Connection With My Subconscious

For a long time, I didn't have good access to parts of my subconscious and intuition, far from the level where I am today. Now, "we" have a strong connection. In my case, there was groundwork to be done: establishing better connections with different parts within myself. I did this with my coaches, who guided me there—some parts needed to be held, heard, and healed. But it was also a matter of insight and practice. Through this work, that connection channel was established.

Another challenge was learning to trust my intuition and

overcome the fear of failure. This required changes in my belief system at the identity level, along with practice to activate new neural paths and connections.

That deeper connection allowed my intuition to express itself more fully: listening to its signals, sitting with certain feelings, acting, implementing, and experimenting. Through this process, my intuition grew stronger. We inevitably make mistakes along the way, but that is by design. These learning experiences are opportunities for growth. Just think of children: they learn to walk by falling down and trying repeatedly until they figure it out. It's the same with your intuition.

Fundamental 68: Trust and develop your intuition through conscious practice. You can meditate or just relax and feel yourself. Interpret inner signals, act and adjust. It is not just about making the right decision, but about building the confidence to act on your inner wisdom.

5.12 Balancing Swift Action with High Standards

Bias for action is one of our 16 leadership principles at Amazon. It means we should value speed and decisive movement over delay, recognizing that in many situations, calculated risk-taking and making decisions with incomplete information is better than being slow or overly cautious. Most times, 80% is good enough to move forward—because most states are temporary anyway, just one step in an evolution. More important is that you take action and progress. Act, take corrective action, win, move forward—and do that consistently.

What happens in reality is that people often spend too long fine-tuning every little detail before taking action, until ultimately, metaphorically speaking, the train has long left the station.

Consider my work with clients and teams at AWS: Do I always take the right actions and decisions? Of course not, although I've developed a strong intuition over the years. The point is, my clients trust me because I actually walk the talk and take action. They know that I constantly move things forward on their behalf.

While bias for action is crucial, two important considerations balance it: First, never compromise your core values and standards. Second, recognize that there are decisions that require careful deliberation—particularly when trust from others is affected, or there are irreversible consequences. In these cases, thorough consideration is essential, as corrective action may be impossible or extremely costly. Remember: trust takes time to build but only moments to destroy.

Fundamental 69: Take decisive action where possible and correct if needed. Avoid analysis paralysis and procrastination, but know to recognize situations when detailed consideration is necessary.

5.13 Environment is Stronger than Will: Your Team for Success

"The quality of your life is a direct reflection of the expectations from your peer group"—as Tony Robbins says. You can have the best mental game, the best systems, and work on great habits. But if your peer group constantly holds you back, you might not get very far.

Your Environment and Peer Group Are Like a Thermostat

Think of it this way: your peer group expects you to be at a certain level, say 70 degrees—this might be regarding your salary, your range of responsibility, the hours you put in, the size of your ideas, or your level of joyfulness and happiness. If you want to increase your temperature, you'll need to put in much more energy, especially if you want to stay there—as your environment is calibrated to 70 degrees. It's almost like an elastic rubber band, constantly pulling you back.

So, how to get to 100 degrees and above? Presuming you've put in great work regarding your mindset and mental health, you've built your willpower and powerful habits and systems. There's one more key ingredient that will determine how sustainable everything you've built is: your environment and specifically your peers.

Your Environment Either Supports or Stops Your Breakthroughs

In phases of pressure and potential breakthrough, what does your peer group advise you to do? Do they suggest you chill, treat yourself with a cheat meal, watch Netflix, and numb yourself with a drink? Or do they propose working out together, going for a walk, meditating, reading a book, or eating something healthy to increase your resilience and energy?

And what about phases of inspiration and insight, when you're about to reach a next level, when you're thriving on a wave of success? Do your peers give you supportive ideas, ask questions that move you forward, connect you with more experts and mentors? Or do they advise you to slow down, not change too much, and stay where you are?

You have to be strategic about who you allow into your inner circle to influence you. Start managing your peer group more consciously. This doesn't mean dissolving all ties with family and friends, nor managing relationships like assets. But you must be more intentional about it—how much time you spend with whom, what kind of feedback and advice you expect to get from them, and why.

Exercise:

1. *Write down the five people closest to you. For each person, summarize in one sentence their expectations of you.*
2. *Reconnect with your most important outcomes in life. Reflect on how your peer groups currently support these outcomes.*
3. *Select three mentors you want to give more space in your life. Create a plan to:*
   - *Be in their proximity more often*
   - *Learn from them*
   - *Get helpful feedback*

Fundamental 70: Choose your environment and peer group consciously. It is comparable to a thermostat that will either elevate you to new heights or maintain your current level.

5.14 How to Build your A-Team for Success

To pick your team—the people in your proximity that support your venture—consider 2-3 key factors. First is their expectations for outcomes, which relates to the above-mentioned thermostat and whether they support your breakthrough. Second is whether they bring capabilities that complement or create synergy with yours, potentially serving as mentors in certain areas. Third, and fundamentally important, is their general mindset and attitude.

Once you've identified these people, some of whom might already be in your life, ask yourself how you could connect with them—or if you already know them, how you might spend more time together. Nurture these relationships intentionally, rather than leaving them to chance.

Be strategic while remaining sincere and heartfelt. Instead of just asking for help, always consider first: what can you give them? Maybe you have specific skills, insights, or connections to offer. Or if you're less experienced, other factors come into play —if you have strong character, charisma, vision, and heart, they may be willing to mentor you. As they've reached a certain level of success, contribution is likely one of their prioritized needs.

Make It Easy, Prepare Yourself, and Take Action

When you approach new people that you want to become part of your team or network, make it easy for them to say yes. For example, invite them for lunch or coffee at a spot convenient for them, and proactively propose a short time window like 30 or 60 minutes. When you already know someone, think of what they naturally enjoy and propose doing that together—whether it's playing golf, running, or doing a fitness workout. After all, a workout is beneficial in many ways and can elevate your relationship to a new level. Pro tip: plan for some kind of follow-up or next step, and be prepared.

Be Responsive, Be Attentive, Pace and Lead with Your Highest Principles

Since my teenage years, I've been proactive about approaching new people—whether at sports, parties, coffee shops, professional events, or the office coffee machine. Breaking the ice can be done in any way; it matters less what you say versus how you say it. Beyond your positive attitude and sincere willingness to learn about others, it's important not to be too intrusive and to give people the choice to engage. Leave them room for a "sweet" and simple escape. You significantly increase your chances of creating meaningful connections when you pace before you lead, for example by naturally mirroring and matching the other person.

While I often learned by doing, the real magic happened when I became more conscious about networking. My best recommendation for networking is Keith Ferrazzi's "Never Eat Alone." My five biggest key insights are:

1. Put **consistent effort** into managing relationships. This is necessary, as it may otherwise fall off the shelf in our busy lives.
2. **Follow up fast and in a personalized way.** For example, when I meet people at a conference, I follow up within 24 hours with a personal message. This 10X effect strengthens the connection.
3. **Authenticity and generosity** are foundations. Focus on creating genuine connections based on shared interests and experiences; look for opportunities to

bond over common passions outside formal settings. Instead of focusing on what others can do for you, ask how you can help them.

4. **Develop a unique personal brand, be visible, and keep in touch.** Stand out by embodying a distinct message or skill. A memorable personal brand makes you more attractive to others and adds value to your network.

5. **Seek mentorship and super connectors.** Find mentors who can guide you and help you learn from their experiences. Connect with individuals who have vast, diverse networks. Such "super-connectors" can open doors to new opportunities and broaden your influence.

Fundamental 71: Build your success team deliberately—seek those who excel in areas where you aspire to grow. Make sure they have a good heart and genuinely support your success. Nurture these relationships and commit to serving your team, at least as much as they serve you.

5.15 Family Dynamics: Choose Your Peers, Love Your Family

Note: This section relates to the family involved during one's upbringing, rather than to your life partner whom you can (hopefully) consciously choose, or your own children.

While you can choose your peer group today, you could obviously not choose the family in which you grew up. When it comes to learning the keys to life fulfillment and success, people may—but often do not—get all the answers from their parents or family members. Even the opposite can be the case: we may take on disempowering beliefs or habitual negative emotions. Or family members may discourage us from pursuing our dreams.

We all grow up in different conditions: financial circumstances, parental emotions, beliefs, values, and habits. Our environment shapes us through various influences—kindergarten, school, sports clubs, village or city life, climate, and whether we have siblings or cousins. Each of us starts from a unique position. Some starting conditions may be more favorable than others, at least at first sight. But we must also consider that it is often the hard times that are growth and learning opportunities that can shape one's character. In a *Hero's Journey*, the *Transformation* and *Victory* are not going to happen without any *Call to Adventure*.

Love Your Family

When it comes to family relationships, my simple suggestion is this: Love your family. Even in cases of conflicting values, disagreements, or past situations where you wish they had acted differently. Others may have made mistakes, but the fact is we all do. Remember that each family member has had their unique life experiences and developed their own perspective on the world.

Handling Life and Career Advice from Your Family

When receiving important feedback from a family member, treat it like any other feedback you would get: as information. Remember that the other person gives you that feedback from their unique perspective on the world, and they may lack crucial information that you have. Although there is always some kind of positive intention behind what a person says (this is one of the NLP Presuppositions), that positive intention may not always be directed toward you. It might stem from self-interest, such as self-protection, like a mother who discourages her child from leaving home to avoid feeling lonely.

Be aware that with family members, we typically let our "shields down" and show ourselves vulnerable, often taking their words for granted. When we are with family, there are usually more emotions involved, which can make information and experiences more likely to stick in our minds - even when the feedback or experience doesn't serve us. It's important to filter appropriately - not necessarily ignoring feedback, but taking responsibility for what you really let in.

Fundamental 72: Love your family unconditionally while honoring your own path. Honor the influence they've had on your journey. Maintain healthy boundaries; you can listen to feedback as information, but decide proactively whose advice you let get through to you and act upon.

5.16 Personal Story: How I Re-Learned to Love my Parents Unconditionally

I am sharing this personal story and reflection, because we often learn from the experiences of others. The same happens in group coaching sessions by the way - not only the person being coached undergoes a transformation, but also the observers if they fully participate. The subconscious will pick up whichever information is helpful.

For several years, I carried blaming and negative feelings toward my parents regarding how they handled their divorce. The way they managed it was far from ideal - which affected me and especially my sisters, who were teenagers during those years. These emotions of blame with negative feelings weren't permanent, but they resided inside me and surfaced regularly. Whenever I got into that state, I would focus on unhelpful questions starting with "How could they..." or "Why didn't I..." The thought spiral would continue, and I would ask myself, "Why didn't I have more ease and joyfulness and just a perfectly intact family?" In moments when I focused on those thoughts, I felt quite miserable. These feelings became part of my emotional home - meaning that I would experience them sometimes, even without an apparent trigger.

When I reflect on those aspects of my mindset from the past, I recognize patterns that are part of a victim mindset rather than that of a leader. From today's perspective, I'd say that my parents undoubtedly made mistakes, but then again, we all make mistakes in one way or another - it's part of human evolution, it is how we learn. My parents had grown up in different times and went through their own unique challenges, which shaped their own map of the world. I am sure that they did the best they could in those moments - they surely knew better, but in times of emotional crisis, they were not acting as their best selves.

Healing Myself and Taking Responsibility

I went through coaching sessions to connect with the parts inside of me that were holding the emotions - clearly there was something to be heard, held and healed. This was one important step; however, after that I still did not fully forgive them. The final step was up to me: I had to take 100% responsibility and make a conscious decision to forgive them. The decision to be bigger than my ego, and prioritize love and gratitude over being right or wrong. That is when the shift happened. I started to focus on what I could influence, and on the positive traits of each person, on all the wonderful moments we experienced together, as well as the love and connection we share. I let my victim-mentality go, along with the heavy "baggage".

That is when I realized that all of this was part of my personal Hero's Journey. Because of this, I developed the urge to become a practical psychologist, to understand how the human mind works, to help myself and my sisters... and then others. Later I realized that these same tools can be used to help people overcome any kind of obstacle and achieve any kind of goal. This developed into a passion for helping people, which started to synergize with other passions of mine - and this is how I started Bright Minds. But it may not have happened if my life had always been sunshine and rainbows.

Appreciating the Time we Have On Earth

We can potentially always find negative aspects to focus on. Not just in our families, but in other areas of life. Each of us has been treated badly one time or another, and yes, some more than others. These times can be tough, especially for a child. However, the fact is that our time on this planet is limited - and so is the time of others. We have a choice: we can either spend a lifetime of resentment, anger or regret, or we can put down our heavy emotional baggage, forgive, let go of negative emotions - and choose a life focusing on the good things: on what connects us, on gratitude, on love.

Then and only then can we see the whole beauty of life, as negative thought and emotion patterns start unwiring. Feeling gratitude for all the beautiful experiences we had, for everything we receive. Only then can we feel unconditional love. It was when I took the decision to forgive that I started again to feel unconditional love for my parents. And I not only chose to forgive them - I also needed to forgive myself and any other person. To make space for unconditional and "unlimited love, inside of me and around me" - as I say in my affirmations.

And in the moment I changed, the whole relationship shifted. I felt more understanding from their perspectives as well - because they probably haven't always been happy about my behaviors and choices either. Now we accept each other's life choices and we are even supportive of one another.

The Key Learnings for Me

Everything that happened to me in life, happened for me. Each experience directed me to seek deeper truths and meanings along my life journey—which has brought so much opportunity, joy, abundance, and new interesting challenges. Today, I'm at peace and share a loving connection with my entire family. I appreciate each one for who they are, and I feel that sense of support - because I took the decision to allow and to focus on that again. My parents are great - despite their flaws. Or maybe because of them, because it made me find a compelling life mission and choose my unique life path.

Prioritizing My Own Needs

One of the most powerful strategies that helped me overcome difficult situations was creating my own "zone" - a personal space encompassing all aspects of myself: my purpose and identity, beliefs and values, strategies, behaviors, and the environment in which I flourish. Like the airplane safety instruction to secure your own oxygen mask first before helping others, I learned to prioritize this zone to sustainably support both myself and those around me.

I've learned to make deliberate choices and stand firmly behind them, even when unconventional. This includes focusing intensely on my mission and career now, while choosing to start my family later. My vision board gives me unwavering certainty about this path. The more I've allowed myself to live authentically on my terms, the more fulfillment I've discovered - attracting like-minded people, generating abundant energy, and ultimately increasing my capacity to give back. This alignment perfectly serves my currently prioritized needs: growth, contribution, and connection/love.

Let me leave you with this: Allow yourself to dream - and take bold steps to create the life you truly want.

Final Words

Congratulations for following through and reading this book until the end. My true perspective on this is: If there's only one important fundamental principle from this book that you take and apply, it can be life-changing. And I've offered you 64 of them—use these success fundamentals to reconnect with these principles frequently and deepen your understanding.

To help you get started, we've created a special 10-day challenge designed to give you immediate momentum. And if you're ready to accelerate your growth even further, consider working with a Bright Minds Coach or joining our *Success Habits Program* and Community. You'll find more details about these opportunities on the following pages.

WHAT'S NEXT

Continue with the Bright Minds Journey

The first step I encourage you to take is applying the fundamentals you've learned in this book through our 10-day challenge. You'll use our simplified accountability tool and follow step-by-step guidance for selected fundamentals each day.

Access the challenge here: www.bright-minds.io/10-days-challenge

If you're committed to accelerate your transformation and truly reach your next level, I encourage you to continue your journey with Bright Minds using one of the options below. We've combined the most effective mindset transformation and success patterns for professionals, helping our clients reach new heights. What makes Bright Minds unique is our holistic approach—we maintain the highest standards in everything we teach, combined with transformational coaching based on Neuro-Linguistic Programming. These patterns were developed by Richard Bandler, Robert Dilts, and Tony Robbins, who have coached presidents, sports teams, top CEOs, and others who've made a difference in the world. I've experienced firsthand how one coaching session can transform everything. Once the leverage is there, we help you succeed.

Here are the three ways to continue with Bright Minds:

1. **The SUCCESS HABITS Program:** A 3-month group coaching program where you experience the content through group coaching and in-depth videos. Depending on your package, you'll also receive 1:1 transformation sessions. These can be at the beginning, e.g., to help you overcome obstacles and connect with your highest self, or during the journey to support your growth and hold you accountable. Readers of SUCCESS FUNDAMENTALS get a 10% discount. You can simply ask our team about it. www.bright-minds.io/success-habits-application

2. **Coaching for Professionals and Executives:** Every great athlete and successful person has a coach. I have had coaches myself for over 5 years, and currently I have three coaches: a Personal Development Coach, a Business Coach, and an NLP Coach/Mentor. You can get coached directly by me, or by one of my partnering coaches. They meet the highest standards in terms of mindset and coaching skills, and these are people whom I initially met and connected with in networks from NLP co-creators and influencers including Richard Bandler, John Grinder, and Robert Dilts. www.bright-minds.io/results-coaching

3. **Team Workshops:** Bright Minds offers workshops and training for teams seeking more than just team building—a mindset shift to their next level. Our offering ranges from formats about vision/mission/culture and the success mindset of an individual, to communication and persuasion. We base our offerings on conscious leadership, success factor modeling, Neuro-Linguistic Programming (broadly), and advanced facilitation practices to create an immersive learning experience. These workshops are

suitable for teams in dynamic environments, whether in corporate or startup. www.bright-minds.io/b2b-trainings-mindset-and-success

We regularly organize intensive workshops, both on-site and online. Follow our social media channels and subscribe to our newsletter, or contact our team directly to learn about upcoming dates. You can find all relevant information and learn more about our clients' success stories on our website www.bright-minds.io

FINAL NOTE OF GRATITUDE

To my grandfather

Josef Hoffmann (born January 13, 1938) dedicated his life to his family while making significant contributions to our local community. He served as town mayor for over 25 years in my hometown and published several books about our region's history.

Josef experienced a great tragedy as a child when his father died from a Second World War blind mine explosion in 1950, just two days after his 12th birthday. Josef was severely injured himself, and after leaving the hospital—with no psychological support whatsoever—he suddenly had to step up and help support his family. His mother, my great-grandmother, found herself managing a tiny agricultural business alone, with three young kids and no other source of income.

Even in his younger years, Josef's childhood was not easy during World War II. However, he developed strong leadership values and a sense of mission, certainly influenced by his father. His father (born in 1899) had been the head of town, chief of the local firefighters, and engaged in many volunteering initiatives. Josef's dream was to get an education, to study, to become a schoolteacher. But reality required him to leave school and take care of his family, providing for their essential needs to survive.

Despite these difficult conditions, which would last for many years, Josef continued to persevere. He became a foreman in the steel industry and engaged in local politics. In 1982, he became head of village, a position he would hold for almost 30 years. During that time, he championed the interests of the people, secured investments, and executed change projects that impacted thousands of lives. He wrote dozens of books and poems to preserve our region's history. He was also an adventurer, and traveled to places like Albania and Mexico, back in the 70s when this was still very unusual. I learned about all of this later, when I became more conscious of it—as a kid, I just experienced him as a very loving grandfather, and the home of Rosi and Josef was always a place of unconditional love. A place of calmness, coziness, and humor.

What I feel like saying is this: the legacy of my grandfather continues to live through this book. And although my mission doesn't rely on just one person or story—this one is worth highlighting, as it touches me whenever I connect with it and fills me with pure gratitude, energy, and love. I am extremely grateful for my parents and every loving person who has played an important role in my life. But this one about my grandfather is a very special one. Life did not deal him a great deck of cards, but he made the most of it. Everyone has their own unique life story. My grandfather is a part of mine - and I am proudly sharing it with you, hoping that it can inspire you as well in some way.

CLOSING REMARKS

I am closing this book with quotes by my mentor Robert Dilts. As he says, the goal of conscious leaders is to "create a world to which people want to belong, including ourselves." And "creating sustainable success is a matter of consciousness and balance with respect to every part of the system, the microsystem and the macrocosm."

Let's be conscious leaders and serve the world.

We may not always succeed at the first attempt, and we may not always do it perfectly. But let's at least do our best, be outrageous, have fun—and enjoy the process. Let's feel that joy, energy and love—and spread it to those around us. Let's allow ourselves to live our dreams—and encourage others to do the same.

www.ingramcontent.com/pod-product-compliance
Lightning Source LLC
Chambersburg PA
CBHW070327270326
41926CB00017B/3793